Studies In the Life of King David

A HEART FOR GOD

GARY OLSBY

Lovingly dedicated to my parents:
Don and Lucille Olsby
Who have shown me through the years
what it means to have a "heart for God."

ISBN 0-89900-735-X

CONTENTS

HELPS FOR TEACHERS

PURPOSE

The first thing that I would stress for anyone that would like to teach this material in a classroom context is to take a good look at your purpose for the study. The purpose for this study is to develop a "HEART FOR GOD" among those who attend. Our goal was not to produce materials which gave more insight into the life of David. Our goal was to produce *character* in the lives of the participants, resulting from the study of the life of David. It's a subtle difference, but at the same time it is a major one which must continually be addressed. It is so easy to get wrapped up with the study proper, and forget the true purpose behind the study. This purpose is clearly, yet simply, explained in the Introduction on page 9.

LESSON STRUCTURE

FELLOWSHIP 10–15 minutes

This is a period of 10-15 minutes at the beginning of each session for true fellowship to occur in a structured manner.

In New Testament times, to be a Christian was to belong to a fellowship of believers who had big things to accomplish and needed one another's support to get them done. Things haven't changed, and our classes can provide this essential support for each student.

Each of our classes should be characterized by its experience of oneness in Christ. We should be developing a "family" atmosphere in our classes. An environment where anyone in class could share a praise or a problem and receive a truly Christlike response from the others in the class.

If we really want our people to grow in the Lord, we must provide them with a group that will guide, challenge, motivate, nurture, stretch, and basically love them in the Lord. Our classes are given the challenge to become such a group. Notice that we're not talking about coffee and donuts (even though these are great). We're speaking of something deeper — of true Christian fellowship, an essential element of any successful class.

So . . . plan activities at the beginning of each session which aid in the development of true fellowship among your class participants.

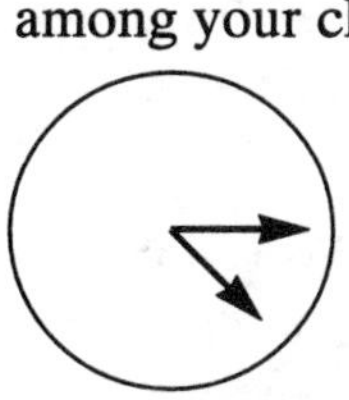

REVIEW 5 minutes

You know, when we teach a lesson, we think that the job is done, don't we? When in reality all that has been accomplished lies hidden in the minds of the pupils, and lies there as a potential rather than as a possession. We want our students to remember what we have taught them, right? Of course we do! Then we as teachers need to take seriously the skills necessary to ensure that our students truly learn. Review, review, and more review! Without it virtually every thought is lost to the learner within a short period of time.

That which is thoroughly and repeatedly reviewed is woven into the very fabric of our thoughts, and becomes a part of our equipment of knowledge. From this firm foundation, then, changes in attitude and behavior are much more easily achieved in the lives of our learners.

From all this it will be seen that the review is not simply an added excellence in teaching which may be dispensed with if time is lacking; it is one of the essential conditions of all true teaching. Not to review is to leave the work half done!

As you teach through the life of David, decide what it is that you want every student to take home with them, to never be forgotten. This has been called the "irreducible minimum," meaning that you cannot take out any of the items to be reviewed without leaving out a major portion of the lesson. For instance, in the study of the life of David, you will want each student to remember forever that David was a *"man after God's own heart."* Therefore, you should review this phrase in some way during all of the lessons.

At the beginning of each lesson, decide which few key points need to be remembered. Stress them throughout the session. Then, after your fellowship time each week, spend about 5 minutes reviewing past lessons. Use your creativity in presenting this material each week.

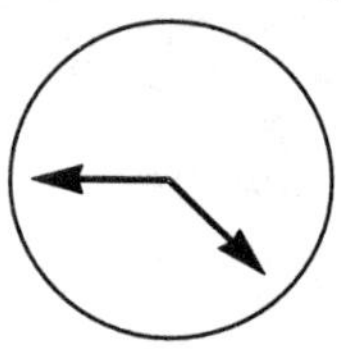

INFORMATION 20–30 minutes

Paul begins his letter to Titus by saying, "Paul, a servant of God and an apostle of Jesus Christ for the faith of God's elect and the knowledge of the truth that leads to godliness." A one-word description of this phrase would be "godliness." Paul tells us that the knowledge of the truth leads to godliness. And what is truth? God's Word is Truth.

Each class session should have God's Word as the focal point of the hour. All that we do in class should come forth as a result of God's revelation to us through Scripture. God's Book is our guide; not our teacher's guide, or the media, or society, or the astrological charts, or even a teacher's opinion. God is GOD — let's remember it!!!

Anytime we have a class where Scripture or Scriptural principles are not being taught and discussed, we are off base; we've lost our proper focus. Let's say to God, with the Psalmist, "I will never forget your precepts, for by them you have renewed my life" (Psalm 119:93).

As you plan for each lesson, figure approximately how much time it will take for "Fellowship" & "Review." Then, plan to spend 50-75% of the remaining time on "Information."

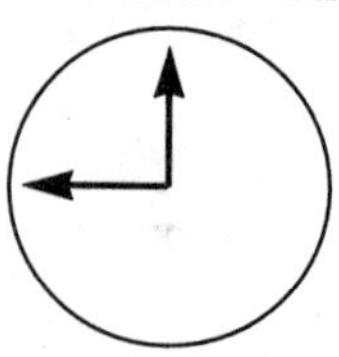

TRANSFORMATION 15–20 minutes

A careful look at passages referring to the purpose of the Bible makes it clear that Scripture was given for transformation — not information! If you question this, take a look: Deuteronomy 6:1-3; Joshua 1:8; 1 Samuel 12:23; Psalm 119:105; Matthew 28:19,20; Colossians 1:9,10; Colossians 1:28; 2 Timothy 3:16,17; Titus 1:1; & James 1:22.

The information of God's Word is indeed our focal point. However, if used properly, it must lead to transformation in the lives of our people. Our content (the Word) is the vehicle to carry us to our destination (changed lives).

To teach in order to merely get across the content could be considered a spiritual abortion — the Word of God is not given a chance to fully develop in the life of the learner.

Now we know why James says, "Not many of you should presume to be teachers, my brothers, because you know that we who teach will be judged more strictly" (James 3:1). But let's not allow this thought to get us down; instead we should allow it to motivate us to fulfill the purpose of Scripture in the lives of our people.

It can easily be seen then that the "Transformation" section in our classroom structure is not simply something to be added on at the end of a lesson. On the contrary, it is our reason for existence, our purpose for teaching. All that we do should lead toward this "Decision & Commitment" time in class. So . . . plan accordingly. Give yourself ample time at the end of each session to apply the information to the hearts of your learners.

MAP SEARCH

The map on page 11 has been provided so that you can plot all of the important geographical movements in the life of David. You will want to do this together as a class. You can either enlarge the map and put it up on a wall so that everyone in class can see it, or you could make a transparency of the map to be used with an overhead projector. As you are involved in the study, and come across a new city, country, or other location, put it on either your wall or transparency map.

Another idea for getting your class members involved in this process is to provide a Bible dictionary and atlas in the classroom during all sessions. When people arrive, they can choose to look up the locations that you have provided for the session in the atlas and dictionary. When you come across the location during the study, you can then refer to those people who chose to look up the references and have them tell the class what they learned about it.

MEMORIZE VERSES

Throughout the study many verses are highlighted which would be very powerful in the lives of your class members if they undertook to memorize them. So . . . why not help them to do so in class? This could be a regular part of your "Review" sessions. Have someone prepare posters of the verses and put them up on the classroom walls. Or, you could have someone print up some computer banners of the verses. By hearing these verses used regularly in class, people will begin to naturally memorize them, and will have more opportunity of remembering them when times get tough.

Another way to help them to memorize the verses is to provide 3"×5" cards in class for all participants. When you discover a verse that is especially meaningful, pull out the cards and have everyone write it down on a card. Then they can take the card and use it for a few weeks to personally review the verse.

TESTIMONIES

Again, we need to remember that our purpose is to create "hearts for God." One way to do this is to put your people in touch with people who have hearts for God. You could bring in people from your own church who have testimonies of the ways in which God is working in their lives since they truly gave God their lives. Or, you could use other resources to make your people aware of the exciting things that God is doing in the lives of normal people like themselves. One of my favorite resources is Chuck Colson's fine book entitled, *Loving God*. In this book, Colson tells many very descriptive and exciting stories of simple, everyday people that God has used and is using to do powerful things for His kingdom.

Isn't it interesting that studying David, who is an excellent example of a man after God's own heart, still doesn't touch some of our people because they think that David is some super hero that they could never be like. By using present day testimonies, these people can see that indeed it is possible to see miracles in our lives on a regular basis.

SING PSALMS

If you have someone in your group who has a gift in the area of music, then please take advantage of it. Many of David's Psalms have been set to music. Find those Psalms/Songs that you think your class would enjoy and have this person lead the class in singing them. What an opportunity to see David's emotions as he went through the events in his life. And, don't forget, music can reach our people's hearts in a completely different way than our teaching, so, take advantage of it.

IN CONCLUSION

Please remember that our job as teachers is an important one! Whenever we teach, our purpose is to affect the hearts of our hearers. What a responsibility! What an honor! Commit yourself to "Do your best to present yourself to God as one approved, a workman who does not need to be ashamed and who correctly handles the word of truth" (2 Timothy 2:15).

LESSON ONE

Introduction

David!!! When we hear that name it usually brings images into our minds of a young man who would go into battle to fight the giant with only a sling. We think of him as one of the greatest heroes throughout all of the Scriptures. And rightly so, for God Himself called David, *"a man after God's own heart."*

One of the most interesting things about the spiritual development of David is the time that it took. God was always working on David. The process was never finished, for David continually struggled with problems. He struggled with his leadership ability. He struggled with his family. He struggled with his pride. He struggled with his flesh. And he even struggled with God's plan for his life.

You know, that's the encouraging thing about studying David's life. We're going to discover that he is just like you and me. We're going to see that he was simply a normal guy who truly gave his heart to God, and therefore God was able to do great things through him. We have the same ability — that's why this book is titled *"How to Have a Heart for God."* Our main purpose is to develop more of our love for God, so that we can have a richer fellowship with Him and He can therefore accomplish more through us.

Wouldn't it be great to someday hear from God, "You're a person after My own heart"? That is our goal in studying David's life.

On page 10 you will find "The Flow of Bible History." This will help us to put the life of David into its proper historical context, further aiding our understanding of his life. If you have used the *Bible History Overview*, you will already be familiar with this chart. If you have not used the Overview books, you may not completely understand the mnemonic at the top of the chart. The capitalized letters in the phrase are the initials of the period headings in the timeline: **B**eginnings, **P**atriarchs, etc. Note that we have italicized the main sources concerning David.

On page 11 you will find a map. We will use this map to plot important geographical information throughout our study of David's life.

Page 12 contains a Family Tree for David, showing his various children with their mothers, and also how Joab, David's commander, was related to him.

THE FLOW OF BIBLE HISTORY

Helpful mnemonic: "BeeP SLoWLy, JaKe CaRRieS CoCoa"

other bible books | **basic bible history books** | **dates** | **key events/people**

Basic bible history books and eras

- GENESIS — BEGINNINGS; PATRIARCHS
- EXODUS — SLAVERY; LAW
- NUMBERS — WANDERINGS (LEVITICUS, DEUTERONOMY)
- JOSHUA — LAND
- JUDGES — JUDGES (RUTH)
- *I SAMUEL* — (*I CHRONICLES*)
- *II SAMUEL*, I KINGS — KINGS
- II KINGS — CAPTIVITIES (II CHRONICLES; ESTHER)
- EZRA, NEHEMIAH — RESTORATION & REBUILD
- SILENCE
- LUKE — CHRIST (MATTHEW, MARK, JOHN)
- ACTS — CHURCH

Dates and key events/people

- — Creation
- — Fall
- — Flood
- — Tower of Babel
- 2100 — God's Covenant with Abraham
- — Isaac
- 2000 — Jacob
- — Joseph
- 1900 — Israelites Enter Egypt
- 1800
- — Israelite Bondage Begins
- 1700
- 1600 — Moses / 10 Plagues / Passover; The Exodus / Red Sea / Mt. Sinai; Tabernacle Built
- 1500 — 12 Spies
- 1400 — Conquest of Promised Land / Joshua / Jericho
- — Othniel (First Judge)
- 1300
- — Deborah
- 1200 — Gideon
- — Ruth
- 1100 — Samson — Samuel
- — ***The People Demand a King / Saul***
- 1000 — ***David***
- — Solomon — Temple Built
- 900 — Divided Kingdom, North: Israel; South: Judah
- — Elijah
- 800 — Jonah
- — Isaiah Begins to Prophesy
- 700 — Israel Is Scattered by Assyria
- — Hezekiah
- — Josiah / "Book of Law" Discovered
- 600 — Jeremiah, Daniel, Ezekiel
- — Judah Taken Captive to Babylon
- 500 — Israelites Return to Jerusalem, Led by Zerubbabel
- — Temple Rebuilt
- — Esther
- 400 — Ezra
- — Nehemiah
- 300
- 200 — Fulfillment of Old Testament — Israel's Messianic King, the Sovereign Servant, the God-Man. Preaching, Healing, Teaching, Equipping Apostles, and Finally Dying for Sinful Men. But the King Left an Empty Tomb and Will Come Again.
- 100
- 0
- 100 — Pentecost — Witnesses in Jerusalem, Judea, Samaria, and to the Ends of the Earth — Peter — Paul.

Other bible books

POETIC (→ I Samuel / I Chronicles era)

JOB
PSALMS
PROVERBS
ECCLESIASTES
SONG OF SONGS

PROPHETIC (→ Kings / Captivities / Restoration era)

ISAIAH
JEREMIAH
LAMENTATIONS
EZEKIEL
DANIEL
HOSEA
JOEL
AMOS
OBADIAH
JONAH
MICAH
NAHUM
HABAKKUK
ZEPHANIAH
HAGGAI
ZECHARIAH
MALACHI

DOCTRINAL (→ Acts / Church)

ROMANS
I CORINTHIANS
II CORINTHIANS
GALATIANS
EPHESIANS
PHILIPPIANS
COLOSSIANS
I THESSALONIANS
II THESSALONIANS
I TIMOTHY
II TIMOTHY
TITUS
PHILEMON
HEBREWS
JAMES
I PETER
II PETER
I JOHN
II JOHN
III JOHN
JUDE

REVELATION
PROPHETIC

"LIFE OF DAVID" MAP

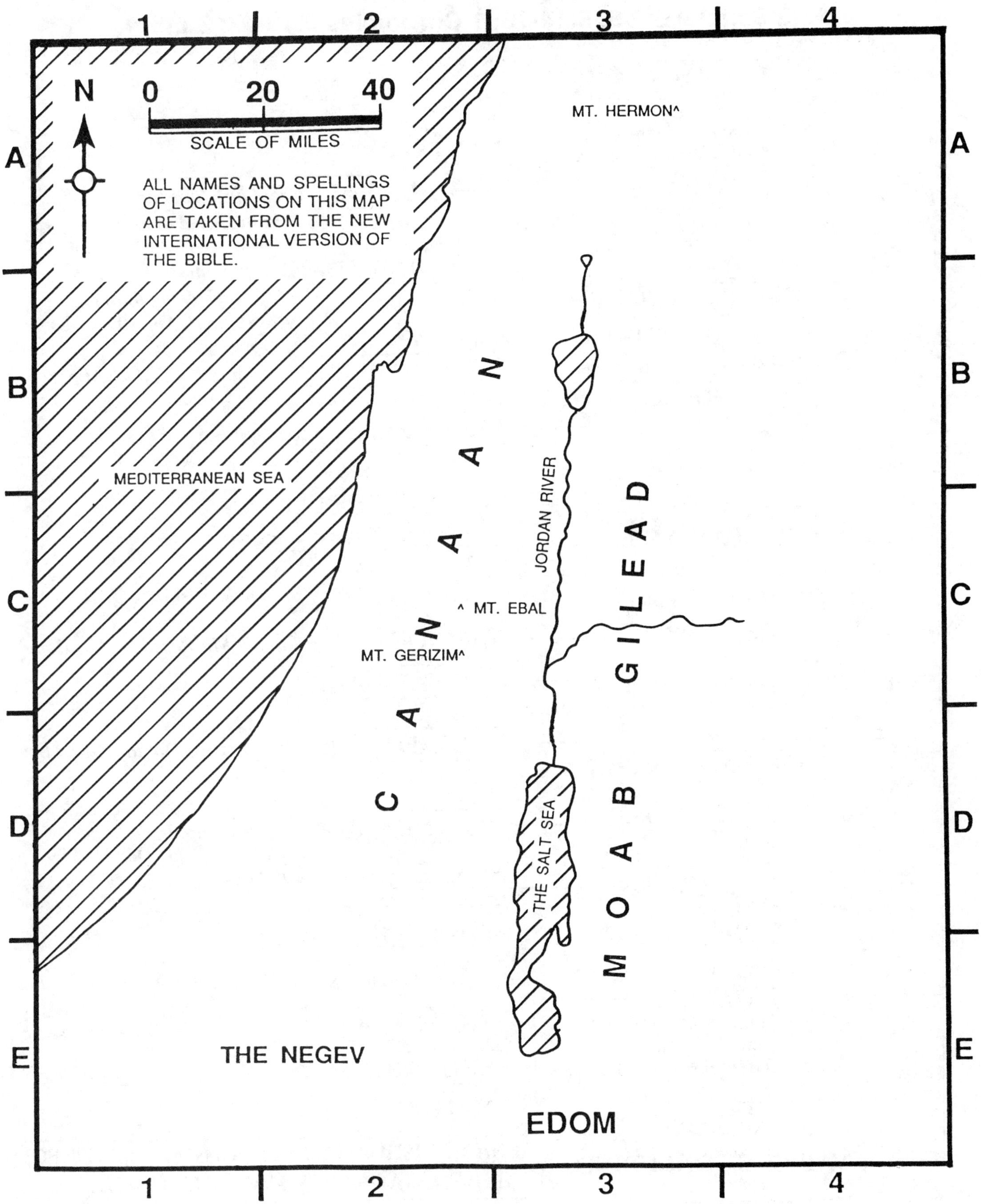

DAVID'S FAMILY TREE

(2 Samuel 3:2-5; 5:14-16; 1 Chronicles 2:13-17; 3:5-8)

- **JESSE**
  - ELIAB
  - ABINADAB
  - SHIMEA
  - NETHANEL
  - RADDAI
  - OZEM
  - ZERUIAH (Daughter)
    - ABISHAI — *Crept into Saul's camp with David at night*
    - JOAB — *David's commander; murdered Abner (Saul's commander), Absalom, & Amasa*
    - ASAHEL — *Fleet-footed, killed by Abner*
  - ABIGAIL (Daughter)
    - AMASA — *Absalom's commander*
  - **DAVID**

DAVID

DAVID'S WIVES	**DAVID'S SONS**	
MICHAL (Daughter of Saul)		
AHINOAM	AMNON	*Raped Tamar; Murdered by Absalom*
ABIGAIL (Ex-wife of Nabal)	KILEAB/DANIEL	
MAACAH (Daughter of King of Geshur)	ABSALOM	*Rebelled against David; Killed by Joab*
HAGGITH	ADONIJAH	*With Joab's help, tried to become king after David; Deposed by Solomon*
ABITAL	SHEPHATIAH	
EGLAH	ITHREAM	
BATHSHEBA (Granddaughter of Ahithophel, daughter of Eliam, & wife of Uriah the Hittite)	SOLOMON	*Succeeded David as King*
	SHAMMUA	
	SHOBAB	
	NATHAN	
VARIOUS CONCUBINES	IBHAR, ELISHUA, ELIPHELET$_1$, NOGAH, NEPHEG, JAPHIA, ELIADA, ELISHAMA, ELIPHELET$_2$	

HOW DO OUR HEARTS RELATE TO GOD?

DO OUR HEARTS NATURALLY WANT TO FOLLOW GOD?

Genesis 8:21 –

Jeremiah 17:9 –

PROVERBS 4:23 SAYS, "Above all else, guard your heart, for it is the wellspring of life." WHY IS IT SO IMPORTANT FOR US TO "GUARD OUR HEARTS"? LUKE 6:45

HOW DOES GOD RELATE TO OUR HEARTS?

Jeremiah 17:10 –

Acts 1:24 –

1 Samuel 16:7 –

Psalms 51:10 –

FROM A STUDY OF THE BOOK OF PROVERBS, COMPARE THE RESULTS OF AN EVIL HEART TO THAT OF A RIGHTEOUS HEART.

EVIL	**RIGHTEOUS**
6:12-15 –	3:5,6 –
6:25 –	10:8 –
17:20 –	16:23 –
28:14 –	22:17-19 –

IN CONCLUSION . . .

Read for the next lesson: 1 Samuel 13:1-15; 15:1-35; and 18:1-30.

LESSON TWO

1 Samuel 9–15

KING SAUL

THE HISTORICAL BACKDROP

Way back in the book of Genesis God had made some very specific promises to the patriarch, Abraham, which were passed down to the entire Israelite nation. They included:

❖ "I will bless you" (12:2).

❖ "I will bless those who bless you, and whoever curses you I will curse" (12:3).

❖ "I will make your name great, and you will be a blessing" (12:2).

❖ "I will make you into a great nation" (12:2).

❖ "To your offspring I will give this land" (12:7).

❖ "Kings will come from you" (17:6).

❖ "All peoples on earth will be blessed through you" (12:3).

God fulfilled the first three of these promises throughout the life of Abraham and his son Isaac.Years later, when it came time to make a *great nation* out of the Israelites, God had a rather peculiar plan. You see, He sent a drought to the land of Canaan on which they lived. Because of this drought they had to depend on the nation of Egypt for their food. However, God had sent Joseph, the great-grandson of Abraham, ahead to Egypt to prepare the way for His people. While in Egypt for approximately four hundred years, the Israelites became a nation of millions. They were so numerous that a Pharaoh arose who feared their strength and therefore made slaves out of all of them. They had truly become a "*great nation.*"

Now that Israel was truly great, God saw fit to give them the land that He had promised to Abraham so many years earlier. Here's where Moses entered the picture. With the help of many of God's miracles, he led the people out of Egypt, their land of slavery. On the way to Canaan, their Promised Land, God gave the people a myriad of laws, including the Ten Commandments, to help them to function as a nation in their new land.

From the border of the Promised Land, they sent out spies into the land to explore it. Ten out of the twelve spies said that the people in the land were too powerful for them to defeat. The people sided with these ten, so the Lord had the people wander in the desert for forty years until all of the adults died and a new generation had been prepared to take the land. Finally, under the direction of Joshua, the Israelites captured Canaan and settled in its cities.

After the incredible commitment and energy that it took to conquer Canaan, the Israelites became quite complacent in their "walk with God." You see, they had everything that they needed. Peace and security led them to depend upon their own strength. In fact, "another generation grew up, who knew neither the Lord nor what he had done for Israel" (Judges 2:10). This led to the nation forsaking the Lord, which provoked the Lord to anger. He then handed them over to raiders from other countries who plundered them. Finally they would cry out to the Lord, who would save them through a Judge. This cycle (Sin, Oppression, Prayer, Deliverance, and Judge's death) continued for approximately 400 years. The last of these judges was a very righteous man named Samuel.

THE PEOPLE DEMAND A KING

In this dark period of depression, brought on by the advancing age of Samuel (1 Samuel 8:1), and the depravity of his sons (1 Samuel 8:3), all the elders of Israel gathered together and came to Samuel at Ramah and asked that he appoint a king to govern them "like all the other nations" (1 Samuel 8:5).

The Israelites had not grasped the idea that they were to be different than "the other nations." The Lord had wanted them to be "a kingdom of priests and a holy nation" (Exodus 19:6), with Him as their king (1 Samuel 8:7), but they couldn't handle it. They wanted a visible military and judicial ruler. Oh, how this reminds us that we are to be "a chosen people, a royal priesthood, a holy nation, a people belonging to God" (1 Peter 2:9). We are to be in this world, but not of this world.

Remember that God had promised Abraham that kings would come from him (Genesis 17:6). The Law even had regulations for the king (Deuteronomy 17:14-20). Yet it seems that the Lord was not ready to fulfill His promise to Abraham. So when the people asked for a king, it turned out to be a negative situation, as the Lord told Samuel, "It is not you they have rejected as their king, but me" (8:7).

The Lord made it clear to the people how difficult life would be under their king, but they persisted. So, the Lord granted their request. He had Samuel anoint Saul, the kind of king that they wanted — someone who could help them to become "like the other nations." Saul was an impressive young man without equal among the Israelites — a head taller than any of the others (9:2). When the people saw him, they shouted, "Long live the king" (10:24). They were so excited about his physical appearance that they thought surely he would be a great success. And for a while he was, for after his first great victory he proclaimed, "this day the Lord has rescued Israel" (1 Samuel 11:13).

But something was missing!

Yes, Saul looked good in the Israelites' eyes. But his height and good looks couldn't hide his small heart, which showed itself in selfishness, egotism, paranoia, depression, and violence. His heart did not long for an obedient "walk" with God. As you read the following passages (all from 1 Samuel) jot down the key ingredients of Saul's rebellion against God.

✐ 10:8; 13:8,9 —

✐ 14:24 —

✐ 15:12 —

✐ 15:17-23 —

✐ 18:6-11 —

✐ 22:17,18 —

✐ 28:7 —

What was the result of Saul's disobedience?

✐ 13:14; 15:22-29

A VIVID EXAMPLE

Let's take a more detailed look at one of the above events (1 Samuel 15). Saul had been in power over Israel for about nine or ten years when Samuel again came to him with a special message from the Lord. The time had come for the Amalekites, Israel's ancient foe, to be annihilated once and for all. Absolutely nothing should be spared. It was a drastic decree that demanded the most implicit compliance. So, Saul gathered his troops, all 210,000 soldiers, and headed for Amalek.

"Then Saul attacked the Amalekites all the way from Havilah to Shur, to the east of Egypt. He took Agag king of the Amalekites alive, and all his people he totally destroyed with the sword. But Saul and the army spared Agag and the best of the sheep and cattle, the fat calves and lambs — everything that was good. These they were unwilling to destroy completely, but everything that was despised and weak they totally destroyed" (1 Samuel 15:7-9).

When Saul returned from this great victory, he met Samuel and said, "The Lord bless you! I have carried out the Lord's instructions" (15:13). But Samuel could see that this wasn't completely true. He basically replied, "Really! Then how is it that I hear the bleating of the sheep and the lowing of the cattle?" Saul decided to pass the buck on the issue, so he blamed it on the soldiers, claiming that they had brought back the best to sacrifice to the Lord. Right! Samuel could see right through his story. He knew that Saul and his men had brought the best back because they wanted it for themselves. And now Saul had the audacity to claim that they had disobeyed God for religious reasons. Wow! What boldness!

> ***"God is far more concerned about character than He is about reputation."***
> **(Briscoe [see references list at end of book], p. 25)**

After a few more minutes of hearing Samuel's rebuke, Saul replied, "But I did obey the Lord" (15:20).

Samuel replied: "Does the Lord delight in burnt offerings and sacrifices as much as in obeying the voice of the Lord? To obey is better than sacrifice, and to heed is better than the fat of rams. For rebellion is like the sin of divination, and arrogance like the evil of idolatry. Because you have rejected the word of the Lord, he has rejected you as king" (15:23,24).

At hearing this, Saul confessed his sin, repented, and begged Samuel to forgive him. Or did he? His words make it look this way, but the Lord knew what was in Saul's heart. He knew that Saul's sorrow was not for his sin, but for getting caught in his sin. Samuel stated, "You have rejected the word of the Lord, and the Lord has rejected you as king over Israel!" (15:26). You see, a man with "heart trouble" can never lead the people of God! God would replace Saul with a "man after God's own heart."

IN CONCLUSION

Do you know what God is looking for in our world today? Exactly what He was looking for in Saul's day — men and women after His own heart! This is not necessarily a perfect heart, as we will see in the life of King David. But it is an honest, genuine, repentant heart! How about you? Where does your heart take you?

What about your desires, your thoughts, your ambitions — the “real you”? Have you discovered some form of “heart disease” in your own life? Let the Lord have it! Spend quality time with Him so that He can create a new heart within you!

Read for the next lesson: 1 Samuel 16.

LESSON THREE

1 Samuel 16

DAVID IS ANOINTED

INTRODUCTION

As we saw in our last lesson, the anointing of Israel's first king, Saul, was actually a negative situation where the people wanted a king so that they could be "like the other nations." The Lord raised up Saul to meet this need in the life of the nation. As you remember, Saul was a "stand out" among the Israelite young men in his physical appearance. They were impressed, and thought that all of their national problems would be solved with a leader like Saul. Boy, were they disappointed!

You see, the Lord gave them what they wanted, not what they needed. They did not need to be "like the other nations." What they needed was a national leader who was totally sold out to the Lord's reign over the nation, and on each individual within the nation. In this way the Lord raised up Saul to be a glaring example to the people of how life would be if they did things their own way. Saul, as the first king, was "the People's Choice." David, the next king, was to be "the Lord's Choice." Throughout David's life we'll have the opportunity to see the striking contrast between these two men and how they handled the problems of life.

SAMUEL'S DILEMMA

"The Lord said to Samuel, 'How long will you mourn for Saul, since I have rejected him as king over Israel? Fill your horn with oil and be on your way; I am sending you to Jesse of Bethlehem. I have chosen one of his sons to be king' " (1 Samuel 16:1).

What a frightening prospect for Samuel, who was convinced Saul would kill him if he anointed a new king. His response to the Lord was, "How can I go? Saul will hear about it and kill me" (1 Samuel 16:1). We would think that this "man of God" who rebuked Saul not long before would not be afraid of him; that he would know that the Lord was with him at all times and had everything in control. But even he wondered and worried about the outcome of this potential encounter. So, the Lord gave him a plan: "Take a heifer with you and say, 'I have come to sacrifice to the Lord.' Invite Jesse to the sacrifice, and I will show you what to do. You are to anoint for me the one I indicate" (1 Samuel 16:2,3).

> ***"We may not know what tomorrow holds . . .***
> ***but we know who holds tomorrow!"* (Swindoll, p. 10)**

Samuel obeyed, and Jesse brought his sons to Samuel, one by one. When Samuel saw Jesse's oldest son, Eliab, he thought, "Surely the Lord's anointed stands here before the Lord" (1 Samuel 16:6).

"But the Lord said to Samuel, 'Do not consider his appearance or his height, for I have rejected him. The

Lord does not look at the things man looks at. Man looks at the outward appearance, but the Lord looks at the heart' " (1 Samuel 16:7).

No, God does not see as man sees. He does not measure character by human charisma. He does not defer to human values. God's chief criterion for selecting special servants for mighty purposes is: "Are you willing to do My will?" This is the acid test. Despite all other abilities, God's search is for people "after His own heart."

Then Jesse had six more of his sons pass before Samuel, each of which was rejected by God. Samuel was perplexed, so he asked Jesse, " 'Are these all the sons you have?' 'There is still the youngest,' Jesse answered, 'but he is tending the sheep.' Samuel said, 'Send for him; we will not sit down until he arrives'" (1 Samuel 16:11).

Why wasn't David brought in with the others? Why was he left to his job in the fields when the others were being considered for a big promotion? We really don't know, but even Jesse's use of the term "smallest," meaning "youngest," suggests that he was totally surprised. Could it be that David's unique relationship with God had brought friction into his relationship with his family, much like that of Joseph years earlier? It's a distinct possibility!

DAVID'S ANOINTING

"When David came in from the hills there was about him a splendid aura of young manhood at its best. Fresh air, sunshine and the spartan life of a shepherd had bronzed his body, hardened his strong muscles and brightened his beautiful eyes. He bore himself with strength, grace, and ease. All of this was bound up in youthful zest and gracious good will" (*Keller, vol. 1, p. 75*).

Scripture says, "He was ruddy, with a fine appearance and handsome features. Then the Lord said, 'Rise and anoint him; he is the one.' So Samuel took the horn of oil and anointed him in the presence of his brothers, and from that day on the Spirit of the Lord came upon David in power" (1 Samuel 16:12,13).

DAVID SERVES SAUL

"Now the Spirit of the Lord had departed from Saul, and an evil spirit from the Lord tormented him" (1 Samuel 16:14). When Saul and his attendants realized what was happening they sought for someone who could play soothing music in order to calm Saul's soul. One of Saul's servants said of David, "I have seen a son of Jesse of Bethlehem who knows how to play the harp. He is a brave man and a warrior. He speaks well and is a fine-looking man. And the Lord is with him" (1 Samuel 16:18).

Now that's not a bad list of qualifications! "David came to Saul and entered his service. Saul liked him very much, and David became one of his armor-bearers" (1 Samuel 16:21). In this position, David would learn many things about being a king and handling the kingdom. However, he would never compete with Saul to try to take over the kingdom. When Saul was depressed, David would play his harp to soothe him. When Saul went into battle, David would carry his gear. But never would David do a thing to harm Saul. As he was a faithful shepherd, now he was a faithful servant to the king.

WHAT PREPARED DAVID'S HEART?

What was it in David's life that prepared his heart so that God would want him to lead his people? What would bring him to the point where God would say that David was "a man after My own heart"? Bruce

Wilkinson (pp. 80–81) explains the companionship that developed between God and David:

> With his flock bedded down for the night, the young shepherd draws a weathered cloak around his shoulders and lies back on the sparse grass of the hillside. . . .
>
> . . . .
>
> These were the nights the shepherd David would never forget. During those long hours of wilderness solitude, HE FELL IN LOVE WITH GOD. And God loved David.
>
> There were probably many in Israel who were faithful to God's commands. . . . and observed the traditions and ceremonies handed down to them by their fathers and their fathers' fathers.
>
> But David's life was different. In David's eyes, GOD WAS A COMPANION. Throughout those years on the sheep trails, David's God emerged from tradition and history to become a warm, personal Friend; one that David loved with all his heart, soul, mind and strength. . . . David learned to relate everything in life . . . to that relationship with his Companion.
>
> . . . .
>
> What a picture Scripture paints: David and God, the young shepherd and the Great Shepherd, walking together through life.

A DISCIPLINED LIFE!

Richard Foster's fine book, *Celebration of Discipline — The Path to Spiritual Growth*, encourages Christians today to exercise the following classic spiritual disciplines that for centuries aided people in spiritual growth:

THE INWARD DISCIPLINES
- Meditation, Prayer, Fasting, Study

THE OUTWARD DISCIPLINES
- Simplicity, Solitude, Submission, Service

THE CORPORATE DISCIPLINES
- Confession, Worship, Guidance, Celebration

Foster (p. 7) explains the disciplines in this way: "A farmer is helpless to grow grain; all he can do is provide the right conditions for the growing of grain. He cultivates the ground, he plants the seed, he waters the plants, and then the natural forces of the earth take over and up comes the grain. This is the way it is with Spiritual Disciplines — they are a way of sowing to the Spirit. The Disciplines are God's way of getting us into the ground; they put us where He can work within us and transform us. They are God's means of grace. God has ordained the Disciplines of the spiritual life as the means by which we place ourselves where He can bless us."

I would encourage you to take a good look at the list above. Are you involved in these types of activities? Think about it! It can make a great difference in your life! As we study the life of David, look for the things on the list — as David practiced many of the Disciplines continually.

IN CONCLUSION

So we have seen that God's estimation of a person is based upon heart response, not head response. Remember always to "guard your heart," so in the times of testing you'll be prepared to say "NO!" One excellent practical way to guard our hearts is to become more involved with the Disciplines listed above. Pick one to work on this week, and make a commitment of time to make sure that it happens.

Read for the next lesson: 1 Samuel 17.

LESSON FOUR

1 Samuel 17

DAVID & GOLIATH

INTRODUCTION

In the last few lessons we have seen how God had rejected Saul as the King of Israel and had raised up David, a "man after God's own heart," to take his place. After being anointed by Samuel we might assume that David would take his rightful place as the new king. However, David waited for God's timing. He would continue to serve Saul until the Lord put him in power.

We might also expect to see a man like David, with his heart secure in the Lord, to have the basic battles of life "licked." "A man after God's own heart" wouldn't have the hassles that life throws at the rest of us, would he? Ha!!! You see, it is important to realize that when a decision is made to truly give God our lives, the hassles and battles of life intensify. The Lord doesn't take us out of the battle, He simply gives us added strength (Himself) to stand strong under the barrage of life.

As we come to chapter 17 of 1 Samuel, we see the Philistines assembling for war against Israel. The Philistines lived southwest of Israel and had often battled with the Israelites throughout the period of the judges, roughly 400 years.

It is interesting to note that the manner of warfare was very interesting, to say the least. The Philistines were camped on one side of the Valley of Elah, with Saul and his army of Israelites on the other side of the valley. Each day the two armies would line both sides of this valley, preparing themselves for battle. In a usual battle these two lines of men would taunt one another, yelling curses at each other until they would finally come together in hand to hand combat. But, there was one thing different about this battle . . .

GOLIATH: THE GIANT

Out stepped this monster of a man. He was 9 ½ feet tall, no doubt a descendant of the Anakim (the giants who had struck terror into the first spies sent into Canaan by Moses more than 400 years earlier). His head, his shoulders, his chest, and his legs were all covered in bronze, glittering in the Palestinian sun. The point of his spear alone weighed fifteen pounds. Goliath was his name.

"Goliath stood and shouted to the ranks of Israel, 'Why do you come out and line up for battle? Am I not a Philistine, and are you not the servants of Saul? Choose a man and have him come to me. If he is able to fight and kill me, we will become your subjects; but if I overcome him and kill him, you will become our subjects and serve us. This day I defy the ranks of Israel! Give me a man and let us fight each other' " (1 Samuel 17:8-10). This happened each day for forty days.

What was the Israelite reaction to the challenge of this man? They were "dismayed and terrified" (1 Samuel 17:11).

DAVID ENTERS THE SCENE

During all of these events, David had been at home taking care of his father's sheep. But, time came for his father to send him to check up on three of his older brothers who were involved in the battle. So, David prepared his gear and food and headed for the army camp. He arrived at the camp as the army was going out to its battle positions. He left his supplies with a servant and headed to the battle line to see his brothers. As he was speaking with them, Goliath came out and shouted his usual defiance. All of the Israelite soldiers ran in great fear.

This whole scene puzzled David. Was there no one daring enough in all of Israel to take on this giant, who had defied the armies of the living God? David simply could not believe what he saw! His heart was stirred! He knew that he must do something about the situation. So, he began his investigation.

He discovered that whoever defeated Goliath would be given great wealth from king Saul. Besides the wealth, Saul would give his daughter in marriage, and exempt the man's family from taxes in Israel. But David didn't seem to be interested in these material things. Instead, his response was, "Who is this uncircumcised Philistine that he should defy the armies of the living God?" (1 Samuel 17:26). You see, Israel was in a covenant relationship with their God. The sign of the covenant was circumcision. David could not understand how someone who did not have a relationship with God could be allowed to stand there and say the things that Goliath had been allowed to say.

> *"If God is for us, who can be against us?"* **(Romans 8:31)**

PERSECUTION FROM WITHIN

David's oldest brother, Eliab, found out about David's inquiries and rebuked him, "Why have you come down here? And with whom did you leave those few sheep in the desert? I know how conceited you are and how wicked your heart is; you came down only to watch the battle" (1 Samuel 17:28).

"What happened to the young shepherd happens all too often in the life of anyone determined to do God's will, to serve His cause. Again and again those who will dare to face the foe, to lock battle with the forces of evil, find themselves harassed by their own family or friends" (*Keller, vol. 1, p. 86*).

The tug at David's heart would not allow him to slow down in his inquiries. He wanted to know who was going to go fight the giant. Certainly someone had the courage to do it!

DAVID PREPARES FOR BATTLE

Word soon came to Saul about David's zeal concerning the situation, so he had David brought in to him. It is so interesting to see the King of Israel talking to such a young man concerning the battle at hand. Hadn't Saul been raised up to "fight the nation's battles?" (1 Samuel 8:20). Wasn't he a head taller than anyone else in the kingdom? (1 Samuel 9:2). Didn't he have one of the few weapons in Israel? (1 Samuel 13:22). And wasn't he of the tribe of Benjamin, whose men were known for their incredible abilities with a sling and a stone? (Judges 20:16). But no, this hulk of a man himself was too much of a coward to think about taking on the giant by himself. He would rather consider a young man, probably still in his teens, to give it a try. After all, no one had a chance to defeat the giant anyway, right?

After trying on the usual battle gear of armor and sword, and discovering that he could hardly move in them, David decided to go up against the giant with a staff in one hand and a sling in the other hand, armed with five smooth stones in the pouch of his shepherd's bag.

THE BATTLE WITH THE "DWARF"

In his fine book, *David —A Man After God's Own Heart*, Charles Swindoll calls this story, "David and the Dwarf." And he is right! You see, David didn't see a 9 1/2 foot giant standing in the valley. He saw his God, his companion, battling a mere dwarf in the valley on that day. David focused on God, not on his own personal weaknesses. Though Goliath was a frightening sight, he was nothing when compared to David's great God.

When Goliath saw who had been sent out to do battle with him, he despised David saying, "Am I a dog, that you come at me with sticks? Come here, and I'll give your flesh to the birds of the air and the beasts of the field!" (1 Samuel 17:43,44).

David's response shows his incredible faith. He replied, "You come against me with sword and spear and javelin, but I come against you in the name of the LORD Almighty, the God of the armies of Israel, whom you have defied. This day the LORD will hand you over to me, and I'll strike you down and cut off your head. Today I will give the carcasses of the Philistine army to the birds of the air and the beasts of the earth, and the whole world will know that there is a God in Israel. All those gathered here will know that it is not by sword or spear that the Lord saves; for the battle is the LORD's, and he will give all of you into our hands" (1 Samuel 17:45–47).

> ***"'Not by might nor by power, but by My Spirit,' says the LORD Almighty."*** **(Zechariah 4:6)**

The fight was a quick one. As the giant approached, David ran at him, slung a stone that hit him on the forehead, and down went Goliath. The Philistines ran, while the Israelites chased them for miles, killing them along the way. David, however, did not pursue the Philistines, but cut off Goliath's head and presented it to Saul.

David wasn't stupid and he wasn't blind. He saw Goliath's size and strength; he saw the oversized bronze armor; he saw that enormous polished sword, glistening in the sun. He saw these things, but his eyes were fixed on his covenant-keeping God. He truly believed that this battle was between his God and Goliath's false gods. The outcome, to him, was obvious.

Nobody thought that he could do it, either! His father hadn't sent him to fight. His big brother wanted him to go home. And Saul sent him out more in desperation than confidence. No! Nobody believed! Nobody but that ONE AUDIENCE, who always believes in us. You see, it's really only ONE AUDIENCE that we live to please anyway. It doesn't matter what people say and think, if it opposes what God wants for our lives. Think about it! David's focus was perfect. His companionship with God directed every other event of his life.

IN CONCLUSION

Stuart Briscoe (p. 51) gives us these thoughts to ponder, "What David was pinpointing for all of us was that individual Christians have to choose whether or not they will champion the cause with which they have chosen to identify. Will they decide to step forward — at the risk of prolonged pain or death — to take their stand? Or will they stay in the trenches? The choice we will make comes down to whether or not we have a heart for God."

So . . . what are the Goliaths that you face today? Are they any of the following:

- ❖ physical limitations
- ❖ finances
- ❖ temptations
- ❖ relationships
- ❖ tough decisions to make
- ❖ fears
- ❖ emotional problems
- ❖ time limitations

Do these and other concerns seem to yell at you across your own valley of Elah? Are you "dismayed and terrified" when you think of them? Take time right now to decide which of your Goliaths you will truly give to the Lord today. Allow Him to be your companion. Let Him have it! Let Him worry about it! And then sit back and watch as He does a miracle in your life.

Read for the next lesson: 1 Samuel 18–19.

LESSON FIVE

1 Samuel 18–19

SAUL'S JEALOUSY OF DAVID

A quick look at the life of David would make it seem that his defeat of the giant, Goliath, was the pinnacle of his young life. After this he would simply need to assume his rightful place as the king. After all, he had been anointed as king, and now he had proven his courage and faith; both attributes which were needed by a king. But a more detailed look paints a much different picture. In this lesson we'll see how David's great successes brought about such a powerful jealousy in Saul that David lost his job, home, wife, and best friend. Furthermore, he had to flee for his life as a fugitive in Israel. In fact, for the next ten years, from about the age twenty to the age of thirty, David was constantly on the move, hiding from King Saul. Before we get into the details of the story, let's take a look at one of David's Psalms written during this time in his life. Read Psalm 59 below and try to identify the stresses in David's life.

1 Deliver me from my enemies, O God;
protect me from those who rise up against me.
2 Deliver me from evildoers and save me from bloodthirsty men.

3 See how they lie in wait for me!
Fierce men conspire against me
for no offense or sin of mine, O LORD.
4 I have done no wrong, yet they are ready to attack me.
Arise to help me; look on my plight!
5 O LORD God Almighty, the God of Israel,
rouse yourself to punish all the nations;
show no mercy to wicked traitors. *Selah*

6 They return at evening,
snarling like dogs,
and prowl about the city.
7 See what they spew from their mouths —
they spew out swords from their lips,
and they say, "Who can hear us?"
8 But you, O LORD, laugh at them;
you scoff at all those nations.
9 O my Strength, I watch for you;
you, O God, are my fortress, 10 my loving God.

God will go before me
and will let me gloat over those who slander me.

11But do not kill them, O Lord our shield,
  or my people will forget.
  In your might make them wander about,
  and bring them down.
12For the sins of their mouths,
  for the words of their lips,
  let them be caught in their pride.
For the curses and lies they utter,
13consume them in wrath,
  consume them till they are no more.
Then it will be known to the ends of the earth
  that God rules over Jacob. *Selah*

14They return at evening,
  snarling like dogs,
  and prowl about the city.
15They wander about for food
  and howl if not satisfied.
16But I will sing of your strength,
  in the morning I will sing of your love;
for you are my fortress,
  my refuge in times of trouble.

17O my Strength, I sing praise to you;
  you, O God, are my fortress, my loving God.

In the space below, list the stresses that you see in David's life and David's response to them.

What was it in David's life that led him to the point where he could say these things? Let's take a look!

SAUL BECOMES JEALOUS OF DAVID

As the troops came in after defeating the Philistines, the women came out from all the towns of Israel singing and dancing. As they danced, they sang: "Saul has slain his thousands, and David his tens of thousands" (1 Samuel 18:7). You can imagine the effect that this would have on Saul. Samuel had already told him that his kingdom was going to be given to another man. God had taken his Holy Spirit from him, and replaced it with an evil spirit. And now he could begin to see the writing on the wall; David was out to steal his kingdom from him (or so Saul thought). "Saul was angry, . . . and from that time on Saul kept a jealous eye on David" (1 Samuel 18:8,9).

The very next day, as David played his harp for Saul, Saul took matters into his own hands. As David played, Saul hurled his spear at him, trying to pin him to the wall. But David eluded Saul.

Saul's next plan was to get David killed through combat. So he put him in charge of a thousand men and sent him out to fight. But David enjoyed the success of the Lord in everything that he did.

When it came time for Saul to give David one of his daughters in marriage (since David had killed the giant), Saul told David that he could marry his oldest daughter. However, he was to fight the king's battles in return. Saul still thought that the Philistines would finally rid the earth of this man, David. But David was too humble to marry Saul's daughter, Merab, so she was given to another man.

When word came to Saul that his daughter, Michal, loved David, he thought that he now had another chance to get rid of David. He informed David that the price for the bride would be one hundred Philistine foreskins. "David and his men went out and killed two hundred Philistines. He brought their foreskins and presented the full number to the king so that he might become the king's son-in-law. Then Saul gave him his daughter Michal in marriage. When Saul realized that the Lord was with David and that his daughter Michal loved David, Saul became still more afraid of him, and he remained his enemy the rest of his days" (1 Samuel 18: 27-29).

Next, Saul told Jonathan, his son, and all of his attendants to kill David. But Jonathan loved David, and told him to hide until he could question his father concerning the situation. As David hid, Jonathan questioned his father the next day. He said, "Let not the king do wrong to his servant David; he has not wronged you, and what he has done has benefited you greatly. He took his life in his hands when he killed the Philistine. The Lord won a great victory for all Israel, and you saw it and were glad. Why then would you do wrong to an innocent man like David by killing him for no reason?" (1 Samuel 19:4,5). Saul listened to Jonathan and vowed not to harm David.

DAVID FLEES FOR HIS LIFE

Again while David played the harp, Saul tried to kill him with his spear. David escaped and went home. But this time Saul would pursue. "Saul sent men to David's house to watch it and to kill him in the morning. But Michal, David's wife, warned him, 'If you don't run for your life tonight, tomorrow you'll be killed.' So Michal let David down through a window, and he fled and escaped. Then Michal took an idol and laid it on the bed, covering it with a garment and putting some goats' hair at the head" (1 Samuel 19:11-13).

In the morning, when Saul's men came for David, Michal said that he was sick. When Saul heard this, he demanded that David be brought to him in bed, so that he could personally kill him. When the servants entered David's house they discovered that he had escaped. To insure her safety, Michal claimed that David would have killed her if she had not assisted in the deception. Meanwhile, David fled and made his escape by going to Samuel at Ramah.

Psalm 59, quoted on pages 25–26, was written during this time in David's life. In fact, the superscription reads, "For the director of music. To the tune of 'Do Not Destroy.' Of David. A miktam. When Saul had sent men to watch David's house in order to kill him." Take a look at the comments that you made concerning the stresses that you could see coming out in David's life. Do you think your comments were accurate? How would you react to these stresses in your life? How did David react? What can we learn from David concerning the way we should handle stress?

IN CONCLUSION

So David was on the run! He had lost everything! His years of enjoying his sheep were gone. His service to the king was gone. His power as a leader among the people was gone. His wife was no longer with him. He would only get to see his friend, Jonathan, a few more times. *How could this be!!! This man had been anointed king of Israel! How could it be that he was running for his life —a fugitive in his own land? Something has got to be wrong here! Perhaps David had sinned, or perhaps God's timing is not man's timing. Perhaps the pitfalls and persecution which David endured were the tools that God used to make him into a great man of God, and leader of his people.* Let's take a look.

> ***"The conversion of a soul is the miracle of a moment,***
> ***the manufacture of a saint is the task of a lifetime."* (Redpath, p. 5)**

In all of our lives, and it even seems like it is all of the time, life throws things at us that we just don't seem to understand. Things that we're not even sure that we can handle. Tough times! And yet Scripture is very clear as to the purpose of these hard times. Read the following verses and explain the positive outcome of these "tough times" in our lives.

✎ Romans 5:3,4 —

✎ James 1:2-4 —

✎ 1 Peter 1:6,7 —

In our society we are used to instant results in whatever we undertake. We want instant food. We want instant service. We want instant solutions. The list could go on and on. Basically, we want instant gratification! And as a Christian, this means that we want instant maturity. We don't want to face the battles of life that produce maturity. No! We want it now! But that's just not the way that the system works. You see, our development toward Christlikeness is a process. It doesn't happen overnight. As a matter of fact the closer that we get to the Lord, the more we realize how far we actually are from mirroring his character.

Think of the trials that you have endured lately, or even those from the past. How did they help you grow? If they didn't help you grow, then did you depend on God to get you through it, or did you attempt to do it under your own power? You see, this is where David becomes a great example for us. Read again Psalm 59. He was depending on God to deliver him, and even ended the Psalm with praise, knowing that his God would save him. With this attitude, we are bound to grow.

On the other hand, if we are pointing our fingers at God and demanding an explanation concerning every part of our life that doesn't seem to work out the way that we think that it should, we will be bitter and still under pressure after the trial has passed. So. . . the key, as it is in so many aspects of our lives, is our attitude. And where does our attitude come from? Our hearts, right? So again we see the importance of "guarding our hearts."

So, where's your heart? Are you joyous to take on the battles of life in the name of your Savior, or, are you possibly looking for those instant solutions that we spoke of before? Think about it! Pray about it! Consider David's attitude! Spend quality time with the Lord! (remember the Disciplines mentioned on page 20).

> ***"No one really advances in his walk with God in a time of complete tranquility. No one develops muscles of faith and trust when everything is prosperity and peace."*** **(Wilkinson, p. 85)**

Read for the next lesson: 1 Samuel 14:1-14; 18:1-4; 19:1-6; 20:1-42; and 23:15-18.

LESSON SIX

1 Samuel 20

DAVID & JONATHAN

In our last lesson, we saw that Saul wanted to get rid of David so badly that he sent men to his house to kill him. We heard David, on the other hand, sing himself out of his problem by faith in his fortress of a God (Psalm 59). But the mere fact that he rejoiced in God has not relieved the pressure at all — in fact, it seems to have intensified.

You remember how David made his escape from his own home to flee from Saul. After this, recorded in 1 Samuel 19, Saul sent messengers three times to kill David at Naioth at Ramah, finally himself making the trip to finish David forever. The story ends with each group of messengers, and finally Saul himself, being held in the grip of the Holy Spirit so that they could not get their hands on David.

After this, David fled from Naioth at Ramah and went to Jonathan and asked, "What have I done? What is my crime? How have I wronged your father, that he is trying to take my life?" (1 Samuel 20:1).

Before we see Jonathan's response, and how he helped David find the answers to his questions, let's take a closer look at Jonathan's life up to this point.

JONATHAN HAD A "HEART" FOR GOD

After David had killed Goliath, and had spent some time with Saul, Scripture tells us that, "Jonathan became one in spirit with David, and he loved him as himself" (1 Samuel 18:1). This literally means that their souls were chained together. In other words, the inner man of Jonathan was bound to the inner man of David. In fact, they felt so drawn to each other that they made a covenant with each other. Covenants were very common in their day, and were taken very seriously. It represented a deep sense of commitment that they had for each other. Jonathan provided the sign of the covenant by giving David his robe, tunic, sword, bow, and belt. As David went out to fight the battles of the king, he wore the gear of none other than the prince of the kingdom.

You'll remember that in our last lesson, Saul actually told Jonathan to kill David (1 Samuel 19:1). In this instance Jonathan boldly came in to the king and questioned him and his motives. At great risk to himself, both physically and emotionally, Jonathan had challenged Saul's conduct. The unpredictable king could have gone crazy over this rebuke from his son. However, God chose to honor Jonathan's courage by bringing peace from the situation.

Why do you suppose that Jonathan and David were so close? How is it that their souls were chained together? Why was the commitment of their covenant so strong? There had to be something very special in common between these two that would lead to such a close and committed relationship.

✐ Read 1 Samuel 14:1-14 and use the space provided to explain how David and Jonathan were so much alike.

David is seen as this generation's hero, but there is no more attractive or praiseworthy model of a godly man than Jonathan. Notice in verse six he says, "Nothing can hinder the Lord from saving, whether by many or by few." Wow! Doesn't this sound like David when he went up against the giant? Oh, yes!

Both had proved their bravery and love for Israel. Both had shown good sense and practical leadership skills. Both were having to deal with Saul, and both saw their roles as helping Saul and minimizing the harm he was doing to Israel. It seems that it never occurred to either of them to form a coup and overthrow Saul, an idea that would probably have been welcomed in Israel.

Do you see the secret here? Do you see what forged their lives so that their souls were bound together? Do you see why their covenant had so much meaning for each of these men? It is simple! They each had a "heart for God!"

> ***"For the eyes of the Lord range throughout the earth***
> ***to strengthen those whose hearts***
> ***are fully committed to him."*** **(2 Chronicles 16:9)**

How gracious God was to give David a true friend at this time, and what a wonderful friend he proved to be!

JONATHAN AGAIN SAVES DAVID'S LIFE

This brings us back to where we left off. We see David asking Jonathan, "What have I done? What is my crime? How have I wronged your father, that he is trying to take my life?"

At first Jonathan wouldn't believe that Saul really wanted to kill David, saying that his father confided him in everything. But David would not accept this. He replied, "Your father knows very well that I have found favor in your eyes, and he has said to himself, 'Jonathan must not know this or he will be grieved.' Yet as surely as the Lord lives and as you live, there is only a step between me and death" (1 Samuel 20:3).

Did you catch David's attitude? Where are his eyes? Are they on God, or Saul? Obviously, they are on Saul! You know, it can be a great comfort to us to see that this great man of God, who was named by God Himself as "a man after God's own heart," could get to the point in his life where he forgot what God's purpose was for his life. We should not use this as a "cop out" to continue in our sin, thinking that if David could not have total victory, then how can we. Rather, we should realize that David struggled with the same temptations that we struggle with. As we sometimes doubt what God is doing in our lives, David also doubted God on occasion. Yet, he was still "a man after God's own heart," as we also can be.

David was determined to discover what Saul's true intentions were. So it was agreed that on the special feast day of the new moon he would be absent from the royal table. If Saul noticed his absence, then Jonathan would state that David had gone home to Bethlehem for an annual sacrifice. Before departing, the two men went out into the woods to reaffirm their covenant to each other. Jonathan promised to tell David his father's intentions. He also asked David, "Show me unfailing kindness like that of the Lord as long as I live, so that I may not be killed, and do not ever cut off your kindness from my family — not even when the Lord has cut off every one of David's enemies from the face of the earth" (1 Samuel 20:14,15).

The very next day was the New Moon festival. And, of course, Saul noticed David's vacant seat. After inquiring of Jonathan and hearing that David had gone to Bethlehem, Saul went crazy. See W. Phillip Keller (vol. 1 — pp. 111-112) who describes the scene (and the events that follow) in a wonderfully poetic way.

1 Samuel 23:15-18 gives us the record of their last meeting. David was at Horesh, on the run as a fugitive from Saul. "Jonathan went to David at Horesh and helped him find strength in God. 'Don't be afraid,' he said. 'My father Saul will not lay a hand on you. You will be king over Israel, and I will be second to you. Even my father Saul knows this.'"

IN CONCLUSION

In her book, *David's Lord* (pp. 43-44), Mary Nelle Schaap points out five characteristics of a true friend. As you look them over, write down how you think that David and Jonathan met each of these qualities.

1. A true friend is unselfish and willing to sacrifice.

2. A true friend is trustworthy.

3. A true friend strengthens and encourages your walk with the Lord.

4. A true friend is sensitive to needs.

5. A true friend communicates.

Schaap ends her thoughts of "true friendship" with these words, "We all need a Jonathan in our lives. Pray for one, and be one in turn! Is your faith in God the central thread in your relationships with Christian friends? Do you turn them back to God? Do you point out His character? Do you allow God to express his grace through you? Those, indeed, are the marks of a true friend."

Read for the next lesson: 1 Samuel 21–23.

LESSON SEVEN

1 Samuel 21–23

DAVID FLEES FROM SAUL

INTRODUCTION

In this lesson we find David running for his life from Saul. He has been anointed as Israel's next king. He has proven his courage and faith. He has shown his incredible talents to all of Israel. He has been totally committed to Israel, and her king. But still, David is running from his enemies and destitute of all his friends.

What a striking picture of the sovereignty of God this story gives us. We know that David would be the next king, but why did he have to endure these hardships before actually ascending the throne? In our eyes it seems a mystery! But to God it was very clear. You see, even with David's great faith, he still had lessons to learn. And these lessons were best learned through the problems and difficulties that life throws at us all. God would keep David safe, but it took this time to show David His love, and to prepare and train him for the responsibilities he would have in future years as a leader of God's people.

Isn't that the way it is in our Christian walk with God? When we set out to develop a heart for God, to serve Christ and His Church no matter what, it is not unusual to find a whole new set of problems — problems that were never expected. We may not understand. In fact, we may cry out to God for answers, as did David. But God is still in charge, and He is allowing our trials to make sure that we still mean business, and to prepare us for future ministry opportunities.

DAVID AT NOB

At the end of chapter twenty of 1 Samuel we see Jonathan and David's very emotional parting. David must flee from Saul! So, he decided to turn to Ahimelech, the priest at Nob, for help. However, his reliance seems to have changed from depending on God to see him through these tough times to depending upon his own craftiness to ensure his safety. He deceived Ahimelech into thinking that he was on a mission for king Saul. First, he demanded that Ahimelech give him food for the supposed mission. Next, he demanded weapons of war. Had he needed these weapons when he faced Goliath in the name of his God? No! But now he acted as if he was on his own. And why he would think that a priest would have weapons is beyond our understanding. But he was frantically in need of security. Ahimelech gave David the sword of Goliath, which seemed to please him greatly. What David didn't realize was that one of Saul's own servants had witnessed this entire event. This would later turn into a tragic event, all because David relied upon his own wisdom, rejecting the wisdom of God.

DAVID AT GATH

David's next plan made no sense at all. He decided to go down and live among the Philistines. But when he arrived they could not believe their eyes. Wasn't this Israel's hero? Wasn't this the man that killed their giant? They could not believe what they were seeing.

When David realized what danger he was in, he resorted to another of his clever strategies. He pretended to be crazy. He made marks on the doors and let saliva run down his beard. Finally Achish, the king of Gath, sent David away.

DAVID FINDS SAFETY IN THE CAVE OF ADULLUM

The cave of Adullam is said to be situated about six miles southeast of Bethlehem. It is a large natural cavern in the side of a cliff. So difficult are the approach and entrance that from within it a few sturdy men could easily defend it. While here his brothers and father's household came to live with him, fearing Saul's jealous rage. While in the cave approximately four hundred men who were in distress or in debt came to live with David, and he became their leader. These men would later form the core of Israel's army, with David as their king.

David's Psalms, many of which were written in this period of his life, often speak of God as the refuge and stronghold. These analogies fit perfectly with David living in the security of the cave. David often began his psalms with expressions of fear, trouble, anger, and discouragement, but invariably before the end, hope had taken over, praise had replaced depression, and David was usually focusing on what God is as much as what God had done. Let's take a quick look at Psalm 142, written while David was in the cave.

1 I cry aloud to the LORD;
  I lift my voice to the LORD for mercy.
2 I pour out my complaint before him;
  before him I tell my trouble.

3 When my spirit grows faint within me,
  it is you who know my way.
In the path where I walk
  men have hidden a snare for me.
4 Look to my right and see;
  no one is concerned for me.
I have no refuge;
  no one cares for my life.

5 I cry to you, O LORD;
  I say, "You are my refuge,
  my portion in the land of the living."
6 Listen to my cry,
  for I am in desperate need;
rescue me from those who pursue me,
  for they are too strong for me.
7 Set me free from my prison
  that I may praise your name.

Then the righteous will gather about me
  because of your goodness to me."

"What was David asking for in this prayer? He was longing with all his heart to know that God was with him. He knew he had not faced Goliath alone, and he knew that he had not won military battles or escaped from Saul alone. Now he desperately needed God's assurance that he did not have to face the isolation in that cave alone. God delights in answering that kind of sincere prayer from His children, and God's presence became very real to David" (*Mary Nelle Schaap, p. 55*).

> ***"Being a person after God's heart doesn't mean never experiencing the concentration camp or the despair of the cave. It means being able to sing in the silent darkness like David did, confident that one day God will deal bountifully with you again."* (Swindoll, p. 46)**

From the cave of Adullum, David traveled to Moab to ask the king to take care of his family. The king graciously agreed. So David left Moab and headed for the forest of Hereth, in the land of Judah. It was while David was in the forest of Hereth that Saul's servant reported what he had seen at Nob (the priest Ahimelech aiding David). Saul summoned the entire group of priests from Nob to come to him at Gibeah. After questioning Ahimelech, and believing that he and his associates were traitors, Saul ordered his guards to execute all of them. When they refused, he allowed Doeg, the servant who had witnessed the events at Nob, to execute all 85 of them. However, Abiathar, the son of Ahimelech, escaped and fled to David.

DAVID SAVES KEILAH

David learned that the Philistines were fighting against Keilah, a city in Judah. He inquired of the Lord, who told him to go fight the Philistines and save Keilah, which David did. However, Saul found out that David was at Keilah. He thought that David had imprisoned himself by entering a city with gates and bars, so he gathered his forces to fight David and his men.

When David learned that Saul was plotting against him, he inquired of the Lord, who told him that the inhabitants of the city would turn him over to Saul. What ingratitude! He had just saved their city against the Philistines, and now David learned that they would turn on him if they felt the need. It is noteworthy to see that David made no attempt to avenge himself on Keilah. Lesser men would have plundered the town in a towering rage.

David and his men, now about six hundred in number, left Keilah and kept moving from place to place. While in the Desert of Ziph his covenanted friend, Jonathan, came to him to help him find strength in his God. What a noble friend! It can be said that Jonathan had achieved the loftiest service any man can attain in life, for he had strengthened his friend's faith in God. Neither of them knew it, but they would never, ever, meet again.

The Ziphites had their own plan. They went to Saul at Gibeah and said that they would give David over to him. Upon being certain where David was, Saul and his men began the search. "Saul was going along one side of the mountain, and David and his men were on the other side, hurrying to get away from Saul. As Saul and his forces were closing in on David and his men to capture them, a messenger came to Saul, saying, 'Come quickly! The Philistines are raiding the land.' Then Saul broke off his pursuit of David and went to meet the Philistines" (1 Samuel 23:26-28).

Wow! Certainly a close call for David! Only God's direct intervention had spared David from certain death. Such divine help came to David, not because he was a faultless man (he was far from it), but because he was a man who above all else wished to do God's will.

> ***"This poor man called, and the Lord heard him;
he saved him out of all his troubles"* (David, Psalm 34:6).**

Review the highlights of this lesson by following David's travels on the following map.

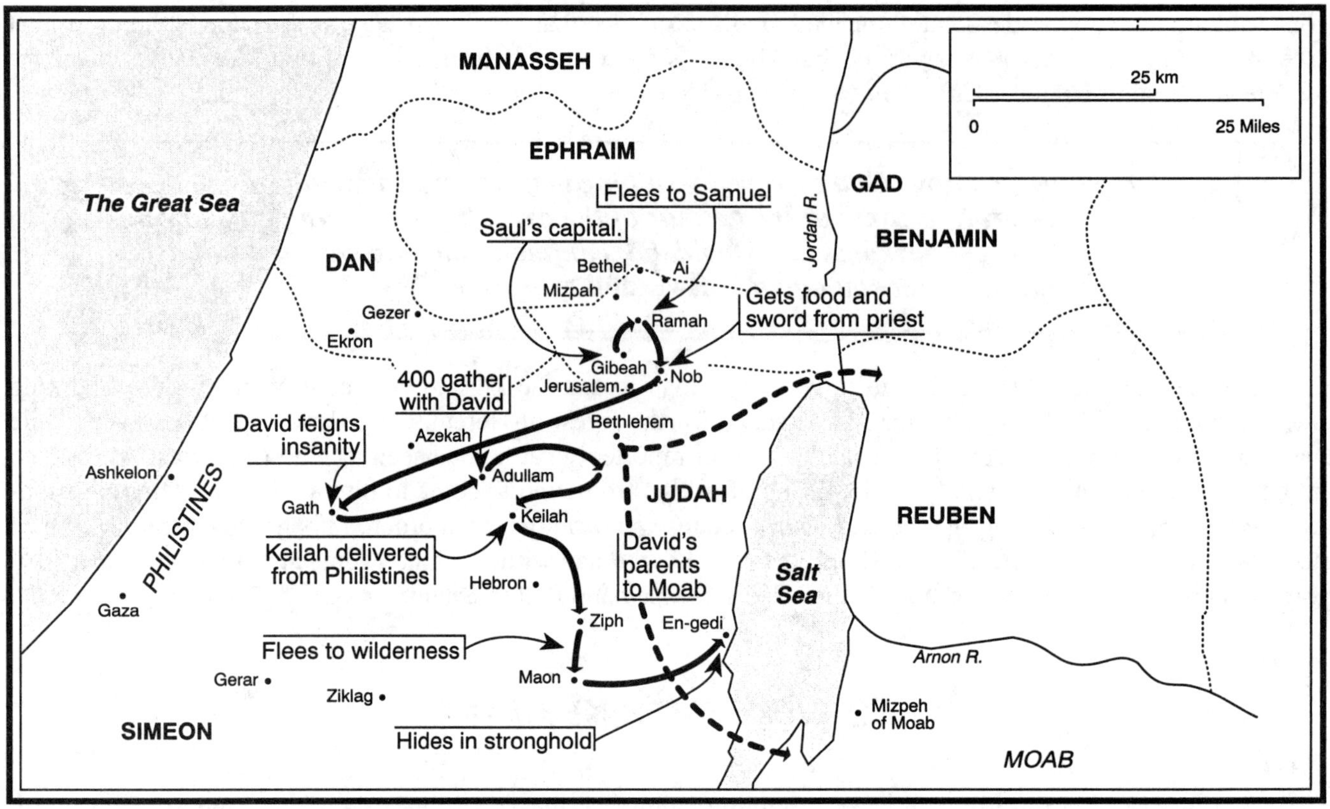

DAVID'S EARLY WANDERINGS
Adapted from *Old Testament History* by Charles F. Pfeiffer

IN CONCLUSION

Chuck Swindoll was once asked (*Smalley & Trent, pp. 129-130*) what his secret is to communicating so much genuine love for those in his flock.

> Dr. Swindoll paused and wrinkled his brow. Finally, after a few moments, he gave a one-word answer: "Pain." Then he spoke of the pain of nearly losing his granddaughter, of doing funerals for too many close friends, of pouring his heart into people who wouldn't listen to Biblical counsel, and of receiving unjustified criticism. Going through pain will make us either bitter or better. Charles Swindoll's trials have deepened and softened his love for Christ and for others.

David knew pain intimately! How about you? What is God teaching you through the trials that He brings your way? Are you bitter or better because of them? What's the verdict?

Read for the next lesson: 1 Samuel 24.

LESSON EIGHT

1 Samuel 24

DAVID SPARES SAUL'S LIFE

INTRODUCTION

As we begin this lesson we again need to be reminded that our growth in the Lord is a process. We don't just simply wake up one morning with a pure and complete maturity in Christ. It takes time! We've seen in past lessons that the trials and tough times that we face in life can actually aid us in this process. They test our faith, so that it can prove itself strong, and we can grow through the process. So, when we ask ourselves why God is allowing David to be hounded by Saul, we are reminded that there is always a purpose behind the events of life; for David, and yes, for us also.

Think of those things in your life right now that could be considered trials. Are you allowing them to help your growth process, or are you rebelling against the potential positive outcome in your life? David's faith and character were molded during these years of persecution. Keep these thoughts in your mind as you study the passage involved in this study.

> ***"Those who trust the Most High to direct their affairs often have to wait long and patiently for Him to accomplish His work behind the scenes. He is not in a great hurry as we are."* (Keller, vol. 2, p. 246)**

DAVID'S BIG TEST

David had gone through many trials and testings by the time he went to En Gedi (1 Samuel 23:29). Now, in 1 Samuel 24, David faced one of his greatest tests. En Gedi was a very mountainous area southwest of the Dead Sea in which were many caves and great rocks, and there David and his men were hiding from Saul.

In an incredible turn of events, Saul, needing to "relieve himself," chose to enter the very cave in which David and his men were hiding. Coincidence? No way! God had the entire situation in His control.

David's men couldn't believe their eyes! What an opportunity! They told David, "This is the very day the Lord spoke of when he said to you, 'I will give your enemy into your hands for you to deal with as you wish'" (1 Samuel 24:4). You can imagine with what intensity they watched their leader slip stealthily toward Saul. Imagine their amazement when David just cut off a corner of Saul's robe, quietly returning to his hiding place in the darkness. They had wanted revenge, but David rebuked them by saying, "The LORD forbid that I should do such a thing to my master, the LORD's anointed, or lift my hand against him; for he is the anointed of the LORD" (1 Samuel 24:6).

Notice that David's men knew that the Lord had brought Saul into the cave that day. However, what they assumed as God's will turned out to be far from the truth, according to David. They wanted David to kill Saul, but David said, in effect, "No way!" Isn't it interesting how easily we can take a situation and know that God wants us to do a certain thing. We justify it as "God's will," or "God's plan for my life." But we haven't checked with God about it. We want it so badly that we justify it as God's will. I recently heard of a young Bible college student who was purchasing an item from a vending machine when all of a sudden the machine emptied itself of all of the money inside it. He walked away with a sizable amount of money, claiming that it was God's way of meeting his needs. Either he didn't care, or he was too blind to see that he was stealing from the owner of the machine.

> ***"Like David, are you bold enough to stand up for your convictions—even when those in your office, family, or neighborhood strongly oppose them? Why not challenge them to godly living by your example? Nothing preachy. Nothing pushy. Just clean, sincere living. God honors those who stand up for His principles. And who knows, because of your godly lifestyle, others just might be persuaded to stand with you."*** **(Swindoll, p. 53)**

Notice also what a sensitive conscience David possessed. As soon as he had cut Saul's robe, God pricked his conscience. He was ashamed that he had even done the little that he had done to insult his king. He knew that this had more to do with his relationship with God than it did with his relationship with Saul. You see, God had placed Saul on the throne, and for reasons of His own was allowing Saul to continue as king. By spoiling Saul's robe, which was a symbol of his position, David was beginning to take things into his own hands, instead of allowing God to take care of the situation. In David's mind, he had sinned, and his heart was torn because of it. Oh, to have such a God honoring, sensitive heart, that would point out even the small sins in our lives!!!

DAVID CONFRONTS SAUL

When Saul eventually left the cave, David ran after him into the open, bowed before him, and confronted him with the irrefutable evidence of his mercy. In effect he told Saul, "Why do you listen to others' rumors about me when you can now see that I mean you no harm? I am guilty of no wrongdoing or rebellion against you, nor will I ever be. I am as helpless as a dead dog and as hard to catch as a flea. May the Lord himself judge between us."

Saul was awestruck. He burst into tears, and cried out, "You are more righteous than I. You have treated me well, but I have treated you badly . . . I know that you will surely be king and that the kingdom of Israel will be established in your hands. Now swear to me by the LORD that you will not cut off my descendants or wipe out my name from my father's family" (1 Samuel 24:17-21). So, David gave his oath to Saul.

Saul was a pitiful man. Here, when his emotions took over, he honestly repented of the wrongs that he had done to David over the years. But, where's the change? Do you think that Saul would stick with this new commitment? Do you think it was safe for David to go home? He sure didn't think so. He and his men continued to live out in the desert, waiting for the day when it truly was safe to go home. You see, Saul was like so many people that we know today who understand the truths about God and what He has done for them, but it's a mere mental assent, not the commitment to obedience that God is truly looking for in people's lives. Their old, selfish, evil ways persist. There is no true conversion — no true turning to God, asking Him to control their lives. This is the striking contrast between Saul and David. One knew that there was a God. The other loved and lived for his covenant-keeping God and Friend.

INJUSTICE TODAY

Injustice is one of the hardest things to endure in life today. It seems that everything within us is screaming out for justice. It is so frustrating to see wicked people prosper while honest people suffer. The Lord has got to have a message for us today on how to handle injustice. Look up the following verses and jot down the key ingredients from each one concerning injustice.

✐ **Deuteronomy 32:35 —**

✐ **Proverbs 20:22 —**

✐ **Matthew 5:38-42 —**

✐ **Matthew 5:43-48 —**

✐ **Romans 12:14-21 —**

✐ **1 Corinthians 6:7 —**

✐ **1 Thessalonians 5:15 —**

✐ **1 Peter 2:19-23 —**

When injustice happens, our inner call for justice can easily lead to "revenge." How easy it is to take the initiative, how hard to wait for God. How painful the circumstances seem, but, oh how much more painful are the consequences of living life outside of God's will.

OK, let's face it! Our society leads us directly opposite of this Scriptural principle. It is tough at times. But what principles of action has God given us in dealing with people of injustice? Let's take a look. Again, jot down your findings in the space provided.

✐ **Matthew 18:21-35 —**

✐ **Luke 11:4 —**

✐ **Ephesians 4:32 —**

How can we continue with the philosophy of life which believes in "My Rights," or "Justified Retaliation"? It's just not right, folks! Did you notice that the above passages make it clear that God's forgiveness is the foundation of our relationship with Him and with others? You see, pondering what it cost God to forgive us makes it much easier to consider forgiving someone who has wronged us.

OK!!! The moment of truth! Honestly judge yourself on this issue. On a scale of 1 (Saul) — 10 (David), how would you rate in truly letting God handle the injustices in your life? Now, what do you need to do about it? Do you need to pray about it? Do you need to study more, so that your convictions can be even stronger? Do you need to ask someone to forgive you for your terrible attitude toward them in the past? Whatever it is: JUST DO IT!!!

Read for the next lesson: 1 Samuel 25.

LESSON NINE

1 Samuel 25

DAVID ACCEPTS CORRECTION

In our last lesson we saw very clearly that God does not want us to repay others for the wicked deeds that they do to us. He has told us; "It is mine to avenge, I will repay" (Deuteronomy 32:35), "Love your enemies" (Matthew 5:44), "Do not take revenge" (Romans 12:19), and "Make sure that nobody pays back wrong for wrong" (1 Thessalonians 5:15). What a great picture of this in practice we saw as David would not harm Saul, although he had a perfect opportunity and Saul was definitely deserving of David's revenge.

Still, within us there is this nagging feeling that there are plenty of times when our own revenge is justified. We can think of times when we retaliated and could honestly say that it was the right thing to do. But, was it? We say, "What was I supposed to do, just sit there and take it?" And we justify our actions by what another person has done to us instead of comparing our actions to God's Word. Now don't get me wrong, I'm not saying that we should be a doormat for everyone to walk all over. But in this area of revenge we need to take a hard look at what God would want from us.

When we compare our actions to David's, some of us may be thinking, "Boy, I could never be like David." But, guess again, for in this lesson David will forget God's principles and take things into his own hands. David, "a *man after God's own heart*," would seek to avenge himself on another. How could this be? It's simple! You see, David was just like you and me; one moment he was victorious in his spiritual walk with God, and another moment he was a complete failure. Being a "man after God's own heart" doesn't mean we're perfect. No! It simply means that when we're confronted with our sin, we're willing to see it as God does and do what God would want us to do to take care of it. And that's what we'll see of David in this lesson. Let's take a look.

DAVID SEEKS HELP FROM A WEALTHY LANDOWNER

David and his men were continuing to hide from Saul. While in the Desert of Maon, David and his men helped to protect the surrounding farmers and shepherds from the raids of the desert's wild tribes, as well as the attacks from the Philistines.

One day, upon hearing that Nabal, a wealthy landowner in the area, was shearing his sheep, David decided to ask Nabal for some assistance with food and supplies for his men. It was a common custom of the day that at shearing time, the owner would share of his profits with those who had helped to protect his flocks. So, David sent ten men to Nabal with this message,

> Long life to you! Good health to you and your household! And good health to all that is yours! Now I hear that it is sheep-shearing time. When your shepherds were with us, we did not mistreat them, and the whole time they were at Carmel nothing of theirs was missing. Ask your own servants and they will tell you. Therefore be favorable toward my young men, since we come at a festive time. Please give your servants and your son David whatever you can find for them" (1 Samuel 25:6-8).

But Nabal didn't see things the way that David did. He saw his men working hard to finish the shearing process. He saw the food that had been prepared to reward them for their hard work. And he saw that he hadn't asked for David's help in the first place. Besides, Scripture tells us that Nabal was "surly and mean in his dealings" (1 Samuel 25:3). So, he replied, "Who is this David? Who is this son of Jesse? Many servants are breaking away from their masters these days. Why should I take my bread and water, and the meat I have slaughtered for my shearers, and give it to men coming from who knows where?" (1 Samuel 25:10–11).

DAVID RESPONDS IN VENGEANCE

If Nabal had simply denied David his request, or if he had handled the situation with a little more tact and sensitivity, who knows what David's response would have been? However, with Nabal boldly insulting David's position and suggesting that David had not been loyal to Saul, David blew his top. Can you see the blood rush to his head? Can you see the intensity in his eyes? Can you see the veins beginning to bulge from his neck? Filled with rage, David told his men, "Put on your swords" (1 Samuel 25:13).

> ***"David! David! What is wrong with you? Why, one of the most wonderful things we have learned about you recently is your patience with Saul. You learned to wait upon the Lord, you refused to lift your hand to touch the Lord's anointed, although he had been your enemy for so many years. But now, look at you! Your self-restraint has gone to pieces and a few insulting words from a fool of a man like Nabal has made you see red! David, what's the matter?"*** **(Redpath, p. 107)**

So David and 400 of his men (the other 200 stayed back to protect the supplies) made preparations and then began the journey which would lead to the annihilation of all of the males in Nabal's family.

ABIGAIL LOVINGLY REBUKES DAVID

Meanwhile, back at the ranch, one of Nabal's servants told his wife, Abigail, what had happened. Scripture tells us that Abigail was "an intelligent and beautiful woman" (1 Samuel 25:3). She knew that she must do something quickly to straighten out the situation. But, women in their culture held no standing in society. What was she to do? At great risk to her own life, Abigail took "two hundred loaves of bread, two skins of wine, five dressed sheep, five seahs of roasted grain, a hundred cakes of raisins and two hundred cakes of pressed figs, and loaded them on donkeys" (1 Samuel 25:18) — all to appease David.

She traveled with her servants and these goods to meet David, but she did not tell Nabal what she was doing. As she came riding her donkey into a mountain ravine, there were David and his men descending toward her. She quickly got off her donkey and bowed down before David with her face to the ground. With graciousness and eloquence she showed great respect for David, something that was greatly lacking in Nabal's reply to David. She said:

> My lord, let the blame be on me alone. Please let your servant speak to you; hear what your servant has to say. May my lord pay no attention to that wicked man Nabal. He is just like his name — his name is Fool, and folly goes with him. But as for me, your servant, I did not see the men my master sent. Now since the LORD has kept you, my master, from bloodshed and from avenging yourself with your own hands, as surely as the LORD lives and as you live, may your enemies and all who intend to harm my master be like Nabal. And let this gift, which your servant has brought to my master, be given to the men who follow you. Please forgive your servant's offense, for the LORD

will certainly make a lasting dynasty for my master, because he fights the LORD's battles. Let no wrongdoing be found in you as long as you live. Even though someone is pursuing you to take your life, the life of my master will be bound securely in the bundle of the living by the LORD your God. But the lives of your enemies he will hurl away as from the pocket of a sling. When the LORD has done for my master every good thing he promised concerning him and has appointed him leader over Israel, my master will not have on his conscience the staggering burden of needless bloodshed or of having avenged himself. And when the LORD has brought my master success, remember your servant (1 Samuel 25:24-31).

In very little time Abigail had helped David to return his focus to the Lord and what He had planned for David's future. Notice that you cannot find a shred of harshness in her words. They were a rebuke in nature, but were presented in such tenderness that David accepted them as truth. They went straight to David's sensitive heart and removed all of the rage that he had allowed to build up.

David responded by saying:

Praise be to the LORD, the God of Israel, who has sent you today to meet me. May you be blessed for your good judgment and for keeping me from bloodshed this day and from avenging myself with my own hands. Otherwise, as surely as the LORD, the God of Israel, lives, who has kept me from harming you, if you had not come quickly to meet me, not one male belonging to Nabal would have been left alive by daybreak (1 Samuel 25:32-34).

David was so thankful, not for the physical gift, which he seemed to have forgotten about, but for the spiritual gift of renewed innocence that Abigail had brought into his life. He praised God, because he could again see that God had everything in control. We can again see that God is sovereign, and graciously meets every one of our needs.

When Abigail had gotten home from saving her family from being wiped off the face of the earth, she noticed that her husband was holding a banquet for his shearers. He was drunk, so she wisely decided to wait until the morning to tell him what had happened. When she did, his heart failed him (probably a heart attack), and ten days later he died. When David heard of this, he sent word to Abigail asking her to become his wife, an offer that she graciously accepted.

CONCLUSION

This story teaches us so clearly that we cannot depend on past successes to get us through our current difficulties. We still have, and always will have, a sin nature which can raise its powerful head at any moment in our lives. It's at those times when we start to think that we have "arrived" that Satan can have his greatest victories in our lives.

"So, if you think you are standing firm, be careful that you don't fall!"
(1 Corinthians 10:12)

This story also shows us the proper response when God disciplines us. You see, God plainly says, "Know then in your heart that as a man disciplines his son, so the Lord your God disciplines you" (Deuteronomy 8:5). The hard thing to see, still, is why David, the future king of Israel, would listen to this woman. All cultural traditions would tell him to ride by her and pay her no heed. But, his sensitive heart could see that God was involved in this situation.

THAT'S IT!!! To have a heart for God does not mean that we are perfect. It means that we are humble enough to see when God is speaking to us, and to obey. And we never know who He might choose to speak to us, do we? It could be the last person on earth that we expect God to work through. It could even be a wicked, evil person. We need to develop hearts that hear God, wherever and whenever He chooses to speak to us.

While encouraging the New Testament Christians to "Hang in There," the writer of Hebrews reminded them that God disciplines those that He loves. Read Hebrews 12:1-11 and record the principles in the space below that you find that would help us when we find ourselves in a situation like David found himself with Nabal.

Read for the next lesson: 1 Samuel 26.

LESSON TEN

1 Samuel 26

DAVID AGAIN SPARES SAUL'S LIFE

I'm sure you remember that in chapter 24 of 1 Samuel, after David had spared Saul's life in the cave, Saul vowed that he would never harm David. But now we see him again hunting for David in the Desert of Ziph. It seems that the Ziphites were hoping to gain favor in Saul's eyes so they once again told Saul that David was hiding in their land. And Saul was more than up to this new opportunity to rid himself of his #1 problem. So, he took his three thousand best men and went searching for David.

When David had heard that Saul was once again after him, he sent out spies to discover their situation and report back to David. He learned Saul's whereabouts and took one of his choice men, Abishai, with him one night to personally sneak into Saul's camp. As they arrived at Saul's camp they saw what they expected; Saul was sleeping in the center of the camp, surrounded on all sides by his men for protection. David and Abishai quietly crept all the way to Saul's position without being detected. The Lord Himself had put all of Saul's men into a deep sleep so that they would not catch David.

Abishai turned to David and said, "Today God has delivered your enemy into your hands. Now let me pin him to the ground with one thrust of my spear; I won't strike him twice" (1 Samuel 26:8). Just as the Lord had brought Saul into the same cave that David and his men were hiding, He once again had allowed David the opportunity to avenge himself on Saul. But he would have nothing to do with such a suggestion. He truly understood that it was God's to avenge. He would leave Saul in God's hands. His reply to Abishai shows the depth of his heart for God. He said, "Don't destroy him! Who can lay a hand on the LORD's anointed and be guiltless? As surely as the LORD lives, the LORD himself will strike him; either his time will come and he will die, or he will go into battle and perish. But the LORD forbid that I should lay a hand on the LORD's anointed. Now get the spear and water jug that are near his head, and let's go" (1 Samuel 26:9-11).

"Many present-day Christians are remiss in dealing with the matter of revenge. They, like the worldly society of their worldly associates, seek to settle scores in their own ways, especially through means of ruthless contention and reprehensible litigation. It should have no place in the life of God's child" (*Keller, vol. 1, p. 163*). But not so with David! He would allow God to settle the score with Saul. His attitude was like Joseph's. When he was tempted by Potiphar's wife, his response was, "How could I do such a wicked thing and sin against God?" (Genesis 39:9). David felt the same way. He knew that Saul deserved judgment, but that was God's job. If he took God's place, then his sin against God would far outweigh his sin against Saul. He truly had "ONE AUDIENCE," a concept that we were introduced to back on page 23.

David and Abishai took Saul's spear and water jug and went to the top of a hill some distance away. David called out to Abner, asking him why he had not properly protected the Lord's anointed. While he was speaking to Abner, Saul recognized his voice and said, "Is that your voice, David my son?" (1 Samuel 26:17). David replied, "Yes, it is, my lord the king. Why is my lord pursuing his servant? What have I done, and what wrong am I guilty of? . . . The king of Israel has come out to look for a flea — as one hunts a partridge in the mountains" (1 Samuel 26:17-20).

We have all seen people repent only because they were caught redhanded. This is Saul's situation. His 3,000 best men again have seen the faithfulness of David. What is he to do? He does the only thing that he can do with so many people's eyes on him in his guilt. He says, "I have sinned. Come back, David my son. Because you considered my life precious today, I will not try to harm you again. Surely I have acted like a fool and have erred greatly" (1 Samuel 26:21).

David replied:

> "Here is the king's spear. Let one of your young men come over and get it. THE LORD REWARDS EVERY MAN FOR HIS RIGHTEOUSNESS AND FAITHFULNESS. The LORD delivered you into my hands today, but I would not lay a hand on the LORD's anointed. As surely as I valued your life today, so may the LORD value my life and deliver me from all trouble." Then Saul said to David, "May you be blessed, my son David; you will do great things and surely triumph." So David went on his way, and Saul returned home (1 Samuel 26:22-25, emphasis added).

THE LORD REWARDS

It is so interesting to see that David understood the concept that "the LORD rewards every man for his righteousness and faithfulness." The same is true today, however, with a few changes from David's day. You see, in David's day when someone spoke of rewards from God, they were refering to physical rewards. If someone back then chose to obey God, then He would bless them in the physical realm. We see this in David's life. It took a while, but since David remained faithful to God throughout his lifetime, God promoted him to be king in Israel, and blessed him bountifully.

Today, however, things are a bit different. This doesn't mean that God does not bless us in the physical realm. Of course He does! What it means is that most of our blessings/rewards are being stored up for us in heaven. Isn't this what it means when Jesus tells us to "store up for yourselves treasures in heaven"? (Matthew 6:20).

Most Christians today believe that when we get to heaven things will be equal for everyone. But this is simply not Scriptural, for the Bible teaches us that our "good deeds" are creating for us our inheritance in heaven (see Colossians 3:24). This is why even Christians are going to stand before the judgment seat of Christ, so that Christ can reward us according to what we did while we were in the body (see 2 Corinthians 5:10). Therefore, some of us will have a greater reward than others, yet there will be no petty jealousy because we know that there is no sin whatsoever in heaven.

What does Scripture say?

> Matthew 5:12 — ". . . great is your reward in heaven."
>
> Luke 6:35 — "Then your reward will be great."
>
> 1 Corinthians 3:8 — "Each will be rewarded according to his own labor."
>
> 1 Corinthians 3:14 — ". . . he will receive his reward."
>
> Ephesians 6:8 — "You know that the Lord will reward everyone for whatever good he does."
>
> 2 John 8 — ". . . that you may be rewarded fully."

And, finally, let's see what Jesus says in the last chapter of the Bible.

> Revelation 22:12 — "Behold, I am coming soon! My reward is with me, and I will give to everyone according to what he has done."

This concept may seem hard to grasp at first because the American Church doesn't seem to have a well-defined doctrine on this topic that makes its way clearly to those who sit in the pews. But it's based on the same principle of rewards that we use with our children when we want them to do a certain behavior. And we are God's children, so He tells us that if we want more reward in heaven, then we are to do more for Him here on earth. Our motivation for obedience, then, is our love for God and the potential rewards that we can be storing up for ourselves.

More passages for further study on this topic: Matthew 5:46; 6:1,4,6; 10:41,42; Mark 9:41; Luke 6:23,35; 1 Corinthians 3:10-15; Hebrews 11:26; and 1 Peter 3:9.

THE FORGOTTEN KING
A LOOK AT PSALM 13

We are told that this Psalm was written by David, but we do not know when he wrote it. Throughout his life, he had many enemies. I suppose that any of these could have brought forth this Psalm from the lips of David. Some say that the enemy is death itself. Perhaps, but we don't see any enemy as persistent in his pursuit of David as Saul. He relentlessly chased David for years, never truthfully giving up on his goal of destroying his supposed archrival. As you read the Psalm, think of those problems in your life that never seem to disappear, those nagging irritations that seem to pop up at the strangest times; those events which make you wonder if there truly is a God.

1How long, O LORD? Will you forget me forever?
How long will you hide your face from me?
2How long must I wrestle with my thoughts
and every day have sorrow in my heart?
How long will my enemy triumph over me?

3Look on me and answer, O LORD my God.
Give light to my eyes, or I will sleep in death;
4my enemy will say, 'I have overcome him,'
and my foes will rejoice when I fall.

5But I trust in your unfailing love;
my heart rejoices in your salvation.
6I will sing to the LORD,
for he has been good to me.

As we read the fourfold chant, "How long? How long? How long? How long?, we are reminded of those times in our lives when we have felt forgotten, but probably never had the nerve to say it to God. And yet, here is the "man after God's own heart" stating it freely and openly for all the world to hear, literally for centuries. You see, David was so close to God that he could share his innermost feelings and not be afraid of God's response to him. He understood that it freed him spiritually to talk to God about his problems, even if one of the problems was with God Himself. At first this is hard to accept, but when we consider that our relationships with others are at their strongest when we are close enough to tell them exactly how we feel about them, then we can see that perhaps it is true with God also.

When we have these feelings of doubt, we know that the problem is with us, not God. That's why we are afraid to express it to God. However, look back at the Psalm and see how David's honesty in sharing his true feelings with God led him to a better understanding of God's Sovereignty. After he had questioned God strongly, he finished the Psalm by saying, "But I trust in your unfailing love; my heart rejoices in your salvation. I will sing to the LORD, for he has been good to me." It's almost as if sharing his emotions led him back to rational thoughts of God. It's so true that, "In those times when we feel that God is forgetting us, those are the times *we need to remember him!*" (*Allen, p. 161*).

HOW ABOUT YOU?

Have you ever felt forgotten by God? Yes, no doubt you have. What did you do with those feelings? Most likely you simply held them in. Think about it for a moment. If you are married, don't you honestly feel closest to your spouse when you can share anything with him/her without feeling that you will be retaliated against in any way. This is true intimacy! And that's the way God wants us to talk to Him. By being honest with Him, He can help us to deal with our feelings in a way that brings Him honor. So, go ahead, tell God what you really feel. Be courageous and confident enough to give it a try. David came out on top, and I think you will too.

Read for the next lesson: 1 Samuel 27, 29, and 30.

LESSON ELEVEN

1 Samuel 27–30

DAVID JOINS HIS ENEMIES

After years of Saul's relentless attempt to kill David, David finally got fed up with the entire situation, and said to himself, "One of these days I will be destroyed by the hand of Saul. The best thing I can do is to escape to the land of the Philistines. Then Saul will give up searching for me anywhere in Israel, and I will slip out of his hand" (1 Samuel 27:1).

> ***"There is nothing ethically, morally, or spiritually wrong with those feelings of despair that chill us like an unexpected downpour. It's when we run for cover in an enemy camp that disobedience begins."*** **(Swindoll, p. 67)**

David! David! David! Think about what you are doing! Remember your Psalms which make it clear that God is your rock! Remember what happened to you the last time that you went down to the Philistines! (see 1 Samuel 21:10-15). Please, David, don't listen to yourself! Come to your senses!

David's actions at this time in his life directly contradicted what God's will was for his life. As a man of God, David had no right to identify himself with the enemies of God. He listened to himself, not God. He never once reminded himself of God's faithfulness in the past to preserve him. He did not seek guidance from the Lord. He only listened to his frightened heart which had come to believe that Saul would actually defeat him.

Notice also the peace that this decision brought into David's life, for Scripture tells us that, "When Saul was told that David had fled to Gath, he no longer searched for him" (1 Samuel 27:4). Of course he found peace! But does this mean that his actions were therefore justified? Of course not! You see, sin has its rewards. In this case David found the peace that he was looking for. But that's not the issue — the issue is whether or not we have an obedient "walk with God." Drugs bring a form of peace, but look at the consequences. The consequences of sin always outweigh the rewards of sin. It's like war! When we find peace, we assume the battling is over, but it might mean that we've been captured by the enemy.

> ***"You can have immediate peace about your sin. You can feel extremely comfortable and warmly accepted in your disobedience. But never for one moment assume that because you have peace about it and are accepted by others that it is right. What you have is a deadened conscience."*** **(Briscoe, p. 83)**

So David turned his back on God. He had joined forces with the enemy. However, the tragic consequences of his sin will later turn him back to God.

Notice that being "a man after God's own heart" does not mean perfection, it means that a person is willing to repent when confronted with his/her sin. It means "walking with God" in a dynamic relationship that would strive to be everything that God wants us to be.

DAVID AT ZIKLAG

The king of the Philistine city of Gath, Achish, warmly accepted David. In fact, he even gave him the city of Ziklag in which to live. While in Ziklag, David and his men raided many of the surrounding cities. They would kill everyone, and take the plunder back to Ziklag. This way there were no witnesses left to tell what David and his men had done (perhaps David recalled his encounter with Doeg, and the results — 1 Samuel 21:7; 22:18-23). When Achish asked David where he had been raiding David would say something about the cities of Judah and the surrounding area. The naive Achish would believe him and trusted him so much that he added David and his men to his own forces.

What we find here is that David's physical peace led to spiritual disaster. He became a terrorist, and a good one at that. His deeds were far more evil than the terrorist deeds that we see today in the Middle East. And what about his deceit toward his new friend, Achish. This deceit led him into straightforward lying as a way of life.

> ***"It is a most dangerous decision to ignore God's wishes in our lives and choose instead to do our own thing. Such choices are often based on our fears or false imaginations which are not under Christ's control. Wrong imaginations can lead us to align ourselves with the very enemies of God. They may even induce us to resort to the world's wicked ways. Thus we become sinister slaves to sin."*** **(Keller, vol. 1, p. 219)**

THE PHILISTINES PREPARE TO BATTLE SAUL

When it came time for the Philistines to battle again with Saul, Achish was excited to have David fighting with him. However, the other Philistine kings questioned the wisdom of this, saying, "Send the man back, that he may return to the place you assigned him. He must not go with us during the fighting. How better could he regain his master's favor than by taking the heads of our own men? Isn't this the David they sang about in their dances: 'Saul has slain his thousands, and David his tens of thousands'?" (1 Samuel 29:4–5). So, Achish explained the situation to David, and David reluctantly headed back to Ziklag with his men.

Can you picture what is actually happening here? David, the anointed king of Israel, was about to fight against his own people, and therefore fight against God Himself. This shows us just how far David had gone away from God's will for his life. And, put yourself in David's shoes. How would you feel if you had to flee your own country, chose to serve the king in another country, but were not acceptable to the leadership of that country. The three day trek back to Ziklag must have been very hard on David personally.

ZIKLAG IS DESTROYED

As David and his men approached Ziklag they noticed what appeared to be smoke coming from their city. Sure enough, the raiding Amalekites had destroyed the city. They had taken captive all the people, women and children alike, and had taken anything of value as plunder.

David and his men were devastated. They wept aloud until they had no strength left to weep. The men were so angry that they even considered stoning David.

DAVID HITS ROCK BOTTOM

Think about these last ten years of David's life. Think of the things that he had lost or were taken away from him:

Position — After he had defeated the giant, Goliath, David was a man of power in Israel. He became Saul's personal armor-bearer, and later led Saul's forces into battle. And he even had the women singing songs about him.

Wealth — David's wealth after defeating Goliath is not recorded, but it had been promised by King Saul. We can assume that he was given much wealth that he had to leave behind when he fled from Saul.

Wife — He had to leave his wife, Michal, in order to flee from Saul. To make things worse, in David's absence, Saul gave Michal to another man as his wife.

Country — Not only was David running anywhere he could find to get away from Saul, but his own people would turn him over to Saul, if given the opportunity.

Spiritual Leader — He had to flee from Samuel's help simply because Saul would have Samuel watched to see if David would come to see him. After his one visit, he never went back to see him again.

Best Friend — Jonathan was a great strength to David, but he could not come with him when he fled.

Parents — He had to take his own parents to Moab for protection from Saul.

New Country — In this lesson we see that his new country had no use for him either. After traveling for three days, he was asked to return home.

City — When they returned from the rejection at the hands of the Philistine kings, they found their city totally destroyed.

Family — David's two wives were taken captive by the Amalekites. We have no word here of children, but there is a good possibility that he had children at this time and that they were taken also.

Possessions — Think of all of the loot that David and his men had taken in their own raiding parties. He had no doubt once again become a very wealthy man.

Friends — His best friends, some of which had been with him for the past ten years, were now speaking of stoning him.

David, where do you turn? Where else is there to turn?

DAVID RETURNS TO GOD

For the first time in sixteen months, "David found strength in the LORD his God" (1 Samuel 30:6). Wow! David had come to his senses! Finally! Now, what do you do when you finally realize that you've turned your back on the Lord? You pray! David inquired of the Lord to see what should be done, if they should pursue the Amalekites, or not. The Lord answered, and told him to pursue them.

DAVID DEFEATS THE AMALEKITES

David and his six hundred men pursued the Amalekites. However, some of the men were exhausted from the week long trip that they had just concluded and the weeping and emotional distress that they had faced. So, two hundred of the men stayed behind and took care of the supplies at the Besor Ravine. The rest continued their pursuit.

As they traveled they came across a man who had been abandoned by his master, one of the Amalekites. After reviving him, he was able to help David and his men in their pursuit. They took the Amalekites by surprise, and by the next day had totally defeated them, rescuing all of the plunder that had been taken.

On the way back to Ziklag some of the men felt that the two hundred that stayed back to care for the supplies should not share in the plunder. So David made sure that they all got to share in the plunder, a sign that his heart was again back on the proper track.

When they arrived in Ziklag, David took some of the plunder that they had taken and sent it to many of the neighboring cities of Judah.

WHERE DO YOU TURN?

What do you do when it seems that all that you have or ever hope to have has been taken away from you? What do you do when you have been treated unjustly? Where do you turn?

You know, in today's society it's so sad when we see people go through terrible experiences because we usually hear them blaming God rather than finding their strength in Him, like David eventually did. It seems that it takes a special person to hang in there with God through trials. But, you know, this is because we have a warped view of our trials. When are we going to be convinced that it is through our trials that the Lord builds character in our lives? When are we going to genuinely rejoice when facing problems, and see the opportunities before us for further spiritual growth? The Lord takes care of His own! We truly have nothing to fear!!! We simply need to rest on His promises!

Read for the next lesson: 1 Samuel 31 and 2 Samuel 1.

LESSON TWELVE

1 Samuel 31–2 Samuel 1

SAUL'S DEATH

As David and his men returned from defeating the Amalekites, they had no idea what had happened in the battle between Israel and the Philistines. While they were saving their families and goods from the Amalekites, Israel was suffering a terrible defeat. Let's take a look:

SAUL TAKES HIS OWN LIFE

"Now the Philistines fought against Israel; the Israelites fled before them, and many fell slain on Mount Gilboa. The Philistines pressed hard after Saul and his sons, and they killed his sons Jonathan, Abinadab, and Malki-shua. The fighting grew fierce around Saul, and when the archers overtook him, they wounded him critically" (1 Samuel 31:1-3).

Saul now knew that he had been defeated, but there was no way in his mind that he was going to allow the enemy to take him alive and play all kinds of disgusting games with him, so he told his armor-bearer to kill him. But, his armor-bearer would not (like David) raise his hand against the Lord's anointed. So, Saul, with the last ounce of strength that he could muster, raised himself up enough so that he could fall on his own sword, thus killing himself. When his armor-bearer saw this, he too fell on his own sword and died.

The defeat was such a devastating one that the people in the nearby cities simply abandoned them and ran for their lives. The Philistines therefore came and occupied them.

The next day the Philistines came out to strip the dead and collect the spoils from the war. On Mount Gilboa they found Saul and his three sons. They cut off his head, stripped off his armor and sent messengers throughout the land to celebrate their great victory. They took his body, and his sons' bodies, and hung them from the wall of Beth Shan.

THE HEROIC DEED OF JABESH GILEAD

Years before (1 Samuel 11:1-11), Saul had saved the city of Jabesh Gilead from an onslaught from the Ammonites. When the valiant men in Jabesh Gilead heard what had been done with the bodies of Saul and his sons, they traveled through the night to Beth Shan, took down Saul and his sons and took them back to Jabesh, where they burned them and buried the bones.

A LOW MOMENT IN ISRAEL

It had been quite a few years since Saul had become king, but consider what had happened in those years.

The people were so excited to have a king that would lead them into their battles and make them into a "real" nation, with a king to represent them. It began with jubilation and ended in defeat. Saul had not extended the borders of Israel. He had not brought peace. All of his accomplishments were only temporary. How sad, and yet how true that when a nation, or leader, decides to do things their own way, God's blessing is pulled and they seem to struggle just to keep their head above water. Were these people's expectations met? Absolutely not! It's simply because they thought peace was brought one way, and they pursued it, but God's peace comes through other channels. Maybe with David as their leader they will let the Lord truly guide them.

DAVID HEARS OF SAUL'S DEATH

On only the third day after returning from defeating the Amalekites, a man arrived in Ziklag from Saul's camp. He explained how he had witnessed the battle on Mount Gilboa and had actually been the one that had put Saul out of his misery by striking him down. He even had Saul's armband and crown to prove his story. David and his men tore their clothes, mourned, and fasted until evening because Saul, Jonathan, and the army of the LORD had fallen. David asked the messenger, "Why were you not afraid to lift your hand to destroy the LORD's anointed?" (2 Samuel 1:14). David then had one of his men strike him down, saying that his own words testified against him.

At first reading it seems like we have two separate stories here concerning Saul's death. The question remains, "Who killed Saul?" Here's what probably happened. This Amalekite came across the battle and watched as Saul and his sons were killed. Then, later when no one was watching he saw his great opportunity to promote himself in David's eyes. He took the crown and armband off of Saul and began his trek to David. All the way he probably dreamed of his rewards that awaited him. "What would David pay to the man who finally ridded him of his biggest problem? And besides, everyone knows that David is going to be the next king; hopefully he will give me a very prominent position in his new government. Boy, this is exciting! What an opportunity. What a lucky man I am." His entire trip he devised the lie that he thought would make him an important man in David's eyes. Instead it led to his own death.

DAVID'S LAMENT FOR SAUL AND JONATHAN

David, in his own pure way, loved Saul. And we know how much he loved Jonathan. He saw this situation, not as a time to celebrate, but to mourn. Even though Saul had deserved David's revenge, he never would retaliate. Instead, he forgave, and longed for the day when the Lord would take care of the situation. No, David was not perfect. In fact, he was far from it. But his relationship with Saul gives us all an example to follow when we are having a tough time getting along with someone.

> ***"One of the hallmarks of God's child is the capacity to forgive others for their wrongs. This is clear evidence that we have experienced the gracious forgiveness of Christ ourselves."*** **(Keller, vol. 2, p. 246)**

David wanted to have fond memories of Saul and Jonathan. He looked for the positive things to bring to light as he wrote and sang a lament concerning Saul and Jonathan. As you read this lament, put yourself in David's shoes and ask yourself if you could write these things about someone like Saul.

Your glory, O Israel, lies slain on your heights.
How the mighty have fallen!

Tell it not in Gath,
proclaim it not in the streets of Ashkelon,
lest the daughters of the Philistines be glad,
lest the daughters of the uncircumcised rejoice.

O mountains of Gilboa,
may you have neither dew nor rain,
nor fields that yield offerings of grain.
For there the shield of the mighty was defiled,
the shield of Saul — no longer rubbed with oil.
From the blood of the slain,
from the flesh of the mighty,
the bow of Jonathan did not turn back,
the sword of Saul did not return unsatisfied.

Saul and Jonathan —
in life they were loved and gracious,
and in death they were not parted.
They were swifter than eagles,
they were stronger than lions.

O daughters of Israel,
weep for Saul,
who clothed you in scarlet and finery,
who adorned your garments with ornaments of gold.

How the mighty have fallen in battle!
Jonathan lies slain on your heights.
I grieve for you, Jonathan my brother;
you were very dear to me.
Your love for me was wonderful,
more wonderful than that of women.

How the mighty have fallen!
The weapons of war have perished!
(2 Samuel 1:19-27)

SAUL & DAVID: "A STRIKING CONTRAST"

The people had asked for a king so that they could "be like the other nations." So the Lord gave them the kind of king that they wanted — a tall, strong, impressive man — Saul. We've seen the results of this man's life.

I'm convinced that God gave them what they wanted. They wanted an impressive physical specimen to strut before their enemies. Who could be better than Saul? Yes, in a sense, he was impressive. But his credentials were irrelevant to what the people really needed. They needed a spiritual leader. I believe that God was, in a way, saying to the nation of Israel, "OK, here's what you want (Saul)." Then when things fell apart He said, "Now, let me give you what you need (David)." Saul and David are placed next to each other in Scripture so that we can see clearly the contrast between a physical man and a spiritual man.

✐ Look up the following passages (which we have already studied) and jot down some notes describing the differences that you see in Saul and David.

PASSAGE	SAUL	DAVID
1 Sam. 17:20-26 —		
1 Sam. 18:5-11 —		
1 Sam. 18:20-29 —		
1 Sam. 24:1-7 —		
1 Sam. 26:7-11 —		

WHAT ABOUT YOUR EULOGY?

It may seem morbid (even though we all know we'll face death one day — unless the Lord returns), but thinking about our death can be a very positive reflection which helps us to see if our priorities are right.

What do you want people to say at your death/funeral? While working on this lesson, I asked my six year old son this question. He replied, "That I was the most famous person in the world." Oh boy, did I have a great "teachable moment" to show him that being famous on earth won't do us any good in heaven. In fact, it's actually the opposite. It's our service on earth that stores up for us "treasures in heaven." I shared other thoughts with him, like having a heart that is sensitive to God's leading, positive character traits such as compassion and forgiveness. Then he said, "Ya dad, that's what I really want people to say."

Honestly, if you died today, what would people say? Would they speak of spiritual, eternal things? Or would they speak of your physical accomplishments? Would they speak of your sensitive heart, or how you tore apart other people's hearts in order to climb the ladder of success?

You know, although we will be absent, we decide now what other people will say after we're gone.

What will people say about you?

Read for the next lesson: 2 Samuel 2–4.

LESSON THIRTEEN

2 Samuel 2–4

DAVID BECOMES KING OF JUDAH

INTRODUCTION

With Saul out of the way, you might think that David would simply become king right away and that the people would respond to him positively from the beginning. But, isn't it true, that as soon as we think that our major problems are resolved, others jump up and take their place. So, David too had to learn that problems are just a part of life. Once Saul was gone, it just opened the door. It didn't solve all the details concerning his promised kingship. New challenges still awaited David.

DAVID IS ANOINTED KING OF JUDAH

It is very significant that the first words recorded from David's mouth after Saul's death and the related events were words aimed at God. David inquired of the Lord and asked, "Shall I go up to one of the towns of Judah?" (2 Samuel 2:1). David was truly ready for God to lead him and serve as his guide. And God blessed him greatly for it. The Lord told him to go up to Hebron, where, without any recorded pomp and celebration, the people of Hebron anointed David king over Judah.

We need to remember that David's years of hiding from Saul, which probably lasted between seven and ten years, were spent either in the land of Judah in the south, or somewhere nearby. He would protect their flocks. He would protect them from raiders that would steal everything that the people owned. And, while living among the Philistines, David even sent many of the spoils of his own raids throughout the land of Judah. So, these people knew and appreciated David. He not only was one of their own, but he had shown special favors to them over the years. It was very natural for them to crown him king.

One of David's first duties as king was to send a delegation to Jabesh Gilead to bring honor on those brave men who had traveled to Beth Shan to return the bodies of Saul and his sons to Israel. In this David was spreading his political influence over the land. He was showing people that he had truly forgiven Saul, and that he wanted to draw the nation together once again.

ABNER TAKES CHARGE IN ISRAEL

Meanwhile, in Israel, Abner, the commander of Saul's army, took Ish-Bosheth, son of Saul, and made him king over all of Israel in Mahanaim. The civil war that existed between Ish-Bosheth and David lasted for years, with David gaining strength and Ish-Bosheth becoming weaker and weaker.

At one of the battles Abner and his men met Joab, David's commander, and his men at the pool of Gibeon.

They played a brutal game where twelve men from each side would be involved in hand-to-hand combat. The result was that all twenty-four died. This led to an all-out battle, where David's men easily defeated Abner's army. However, Asahel, brother of Joab, was killed by Abner himself.

ABNER GOES OVER TO DAVID'S SIDE

One day, in the midst of this civil war, Ish-Bosheth accused Abner of sleeping with one of Saul's concubines. We do not know if he was guilty or not. The verse preceding this states, "Abner was strengthening his own position in the house of Saul" (2 Samuel 3:6). A king's concubines were considered royal property, and a man who claimed the wives or concubines of a king would be taking strong steps toward taking the throne.

We may not know of Abner's guilt or innocence, but we do know of his intense anger about the situation. He responded, "Am I a dog's head — on Judah's side? This very day I am loyal to the house of your father Saul and to his family and friends. I haven't handed you over to David. Yet now you accuse me of an offense involving this woman! May God deal with Abner, be it ever so severely, if I do not do for David what the LORD promised him on oath and transfer the kingdom from the house of Saul and establish David's throne over Israel and Judah from Dan to Beersheba" (2 Samuel 3:8-10).

Abner sent word to David of his intentions. David basically said, "Great!, but do not come here to me until you have returned my wife Michal to me." So, Michal was taken from her new husband, at the order of Ish-Bosheth, and taken to David.

Abner then spent time with the elders of Israel saying, "For some time you have wanted to make David your king. Now do it!" (2 Samuel 3:17,18). He spent special time with the Benjamites, Saul's tribe, who had lost many warriors to David's army.

Finally, Abner came to David to make the transfer of power official. David did not question Abner's motives, even though this man had hounded him in the desert to kill him for Saul. Again, we see how pure David's heart really was. He could truly forgive someone and forget the past. Wow!!! What an example! Yes, David not only accepted Abner, but he prepared a feast for him and his twenty associates. After this feast, Abner left in peace to assemble all Israel for David.

JOAB MURDERS ABNER

Meanwhile, Joab and many of David's men had been out raiding. They returned with a great deal of plunder. When they heard that David had accepted Abner in peace, Joab was angry. He said, "What have you done? Look, Abner came to you. Why did you let him go? Now he is gone! You know Abner son of Ner; he came to deceive you and observe your movements and find out everything you are doing" (2 Samuel 3:24,25).

Joab took matters into his own hands and sent messengers to Abner to bring him back to Hebron. "But David did not know of it. Now when Abner returned to Hebron, Joab took him aside into the gateway, as though to speak with him privately. And there, to avenge the blood of his brother Asahel, Joab stabbed him in the stomach, and he died" (2 Samuel 3:26,27).

> ***"You have heard it said, 'Love your neighbor and hate your enemy.' But I tell you: Love your enemies and pray for those who persecute you, that you may be sons of your Father in heaven."*** **Jesus (Matthew 5:43-45)**

When David heard what had happened, he denied any responsibility and said, "I and my kingdom are forever innocent before the Lord concerning the blood of Abner son of Ner. May his blood fall upon the head of Joab and upon all his father's house! May Joab's house never be without someone who has a running sore or leprosy or who leans on a crutch or who falls by the sword or who lacks food" (2 Samuel 3:28,29).

Not only did David curse the house of Joab in this way, but he also had all of his men mourn Abner's death by tearing their clothes and wearing sackcloth. David himself walked behind the bier, and wept aloud at Abner's tomb. He also would not eat anything until evening. By these actions, although not put on as an act, David proved to the tribes of Israel that he truly was innocent in the death of Abner. And the people took note and were pleased; indeed, everything the king did pleased them.

ISH-BOSHETH IS MURDERED

You can imagine the impact upon Ish-Bosheth when he heard the news that Abner was dead. Abner had made him king. And it was Abner who had the strength physically and politically to keep him as king. I think Ish-Bosheth was also hoping for Abner's trip to Judah to result in positive relations between he and David.

However, as things progressed, Ish-Bosheth never had an opportunity to settle his feud with David. Two men from his own forces, Recab and Baanah, came to him one day while he was taking his mid-day rest and murdered him in cold blood. They got away from his house without being noticed, and traveled all night to David at Hebron, thinking that David would reward them for their efforts.

Do you remember what happened to the man who claimed that he had killed the last king of Israel, Saul? Well, the same plight is about to come upon these men. When they arrived in Hebron, David responded to their actions with these words, "As surely as the LORD lives, who has delivered me out of all trouble, when a man told me, 'Saul is dead,' and thought he was bringing good news, I seized him and put him to death in Ziklag. That was the reward I gave him for his news! How much more — when wicked men have killed an innocent man in his own house and on his own bed — should I not now demand his blood from your hand and rid the earth of you!" (2 Samuel 4:9-11). Then David ordered his men to put them to death.

IN CONCLUSION

In this lesson it seems that we have spent much time looking at other people besides David. People like Abner, Ish-Bosheth, and Joab. We only saw a few glimpses of David's heart through these pages, and they were good glimpses to see. We saw him inquiring of the Lord at the beginning of the lesson. We saw him showing kindness to the inhabitants of Jabesh Gilead. Later he truly forgave Abner of the years of persecution at his hands. And then he sincerely mourned the death of Abner. Yes, he truly was "a man after God's own heart."

Some scholars believe that David wrote Psalm 101 at this time in his life. Let's take a look:

1 I will sing of your love and justice;
to you, O LORD, I will sing praise.
2 I will be careful to lead a blameless life —
when will you come to me?

I will walk in my house
with blameless heart.
3 I will set before my eyes no vile thing.

The deeds of faithless men I hate;
they will not cling to me.

[4]Men of perverse heart shall be far from me;
I will have nothing to do with evil.

[5]Whoever slanders his neighbor in secret,
him will I put to silence;
whoever has haughty eyes and a proud heart,
him will I not endure.

[6]My eyes will be on the faithful in the land,
that they may dwell with me;
he whose walk is blameless
will minister to me.

[7]No one who practices deceit
will dwell in my house;
no one who speaks falsely
will stand in my presence.

[8]Every morning I will put to silence
all the wicked in the land;
I will cut off every evildoer
from the city of the LORD.

You know, today's society is so tolerant of any new idea and lifestyle that comes along. Quite often we get caught up in this kind of thinking and find ourselves at odds with what God has said in His Word. We buy into false teaching simply because we have allowed that kind of thinking to enter our minds. David has said, "I will set before my eyes no vile thing!" Then he went on to explain that this means not being tolerant of others who speak and do evil practices. Let's face it! We get ourselves into trouble at times because we have spent time with the wrong people. We want to be tolerant of their lifestyles, so that we don't offend them. But at the same time we are being affected and we don't even realize it. When you see yourself becoming critical of what God has said in His Word, it probably means that you've spent too much time with the wrong company. Oh, yes, we are to love them. But we are not to give in to their humanistic thinking. We are to be the "salt" of the world, not the sponge. Are there subjects where you think that God's Word may be outdated; that people today understand better than Scripture? If so, you need to take a good look at where you were fed this lie. And you (and all of us to some degree) need to recommit yourself to God and His Word.

Read for the next lesson: 2 Samuel 5–6.

LESSON FOURTEEN

2 Samuel 5–6

DAVID BECOMES KING OVER ALL ISRAEL

In our last lesson we saw how Abner had basically prepared the northern tribes to accept David as their king. Then, we saw him murdered by Joab. David conducted himself so well during the events which followed Abner's death that the people knew that he had nothing to do with Abner's death.

So, the people of Israel came to David at Hebron to make him their king. They said three things to convince David that he was to be king of all Israel:

1) You are one of us — "*our own flesh and blood*" — We are family!

2) Even when Saul was king, you were the one who led Israel on their military campaigns.

3) It's God's will! He had said that you would one day shepherd His people, Israel.

It is also quite significant to notice the large numbers of people who came to Hebron to anoint David as their next king. 1 Chronicles 12:23-40 tells us that it was virtually a convention of the entire nation, some 350,000 warriors, besides others, came to be part of this exciting time in Israel. The nation was truly rallying around their new king. David was thirty-seven years of age when he officially became king over all Israel.

DAVID CONQUERS JERUSALEM

Hebron could never be the capital of an important and powerful kingdom in Palestine. It was poorly located for the purpose of defense, and it would be unacceptable to the tribe of Benjamin. Likewise a northern capital would be unacceptable to Judah in the south. If the kingdom was to enjoy a stable government, it must have a central capital which could be developed into a symbol of national prowess. Twenty miles to the north of Hebron, on neutral ground between northern and southern tribes, lay the strongest fortified city of the region, Jebus.

Jebus, the city of the Jebusites, occupied a strategic site. It was the focal point where the routes from Gaza, Jaffa, Shechem, Jericho, and Bethlehem crossed. Yet it was remote enough for security. Built on three hills, it had sections of wall 40 feet thick. Even in the heyday of Joshua's mighty exploits in occupying Canaan, Israel never totally overtook it. For well over four hundred years it stood defiant in the heart of Israel. So defiant, in fact, that the people of the city even yelled at David that the "blind and lame" could defend the city against him.

David accepted the challenge, and promised the position of commander-in-chief to the first man entering the city. Joab became the hero. The Israelites had located an underground waterway that opened into the heart of the city. Joab scaled the rocks, wading through water up to his waist, followed by other brave warriors, and totally surprised the defenders.

The city was then given its former name, Jerusalem. In time it was given several other names as well, such as; "The City of David," "The Royal City," "Zion," and "Mount Zion the City of our God." It was also completely independent of the Israelite tribal system. It owed allegiance only to the king!

Not long after David defeated the Jebusites, as a token of friendship, Hiram, king of Tyre, sent David all of the materials and workers needed to build himself a palace. "And David knew that the LORD had established him as king over Israel and had exalted his kingdom for the sake of his people Israel" (2 Samuel 5:12).

DAVID DEFEATS THE PHILISTINES

Throughout the reign of Saul the number one enemy of Israel had been the Philistines. They were Saul's main enemy, resulting in his death. In the seven years since the death of Saul, the Philistines were strengthening their hold on the area. When they heard that David had been anointed king over all Israel they went up in full force to meet David in battle. David heard that they were coming and did one incredibly wise move. He moved to his knees to ask the Lord what he should do. The Lord told him to attack, that he would be victorious. And he was! In fact, the Philistines retreated in such haste that they left behind their personal idols as they fled. 1 Chronicles 14:12 says that the Israelites destroyed them with fire.

Once again the Philistines came up to Israel to battle. Now you might think that David would not need to pray, relying upon God's answer to his last prayer concerning the Philistines to cover this attack also. But David was much wiser. He inquired of the Lord, who gave him a new strategy for this current battle. David routed the Philistines so completely that we hear little of them until David's later years.

Notice how David depended upon the Lord so completely. He could have assumed that God wanted him to go to war with the Philistines, knowing that God had already promised him victory. But No! This was a new day. Although it was the same enemy, it was a brand new battle. He needed to totally rely on the Lord again for the battle to result in victory. He knew that past victories do not assure us success in the present, just as we cannot expect that our past spiritual victories will bring us present victories. We cannot camp on the past. We must daily give God each of our battles so that He can truly fight them for us.

DAVID BRINGS THE ARK OF THE COVENANT TO JERUSALEM

David still had a large job in front of him. In fact, he had hardly begun his most important job — that being the return of the entire nation to the worship of the one true God. But where would he start? Saul had killed all the priests at Nob. The Tabernacle had deteriorated, its furnishings had been scattered, and the worship itself had become virtually meaningless. However, David came up with a simple plan. Since God's presence was associated with the Ark of the Covenant, David decided to bring it to Jerusalem, to become the focal point in the nation's return to God. David no doubt also felt that his personal relationship with God would be furthered with this move. To have "The Presence" so close at hand had to make him feel very secure.

> ***"I often hear others pray, and I often pray myself, 'O Lord, grant me today the sense of Thy presence! Without Thee my purpose faints; without Thee my spirit grows weak; without Thee I shall make so many mistakes and go wrong in so many decisions. Lord, this day I desire above all else the conscious sense of Thy presence in my life.'"*** **(Redpath, p. 158)**

The Ark of the Covenant was approximately four feet long, two feet wide, and two feet high. It was made of acacia wood and covered with gold. The lid was of solid gold, and on the gold lid were carvings of two cherubim that faced each other. Four rings were placed on the sides of the Ark, and poles were placed through the rings for use in carrying the Ark. It denoted the very Presence of God; it bore the covenant promises of power vested in Him. It was the place of pardon and peace where the Almighty met with men at the sacred mercy-seat. It bore the Law of God. The Ark had been kept in the household of Abinadab in Kiriath Jearim for years, from where David wanted to rescue it and put it in a place of honor that it deserved.

David assembled some 30,000 representatives from all over Israel to participate in this celebration. There was a massed choir of voices plus a huge orchestra of musicians playing songs of praise on every sort of instrument. They placed the Ark on a new cart and began the trip to Jerusalem. Abinadab's own sons, Uzzah and Ahio, were guiding the cart. Suddenly, the oxen stumbled. Uzzah reached out to steady the Ark with his hand. He fell dead instantly! With the best of intentions, Uzzah had ignored the clear and explicit edict to never touch the Ark (Numbers 4:15).

> ***"All the planning; all the programs; all the praise and dramatic displays of man's devising come to nothing if they are not in clear compliance with our Father's will and instructions to us."*** **(Keller, vol. 2, p. 53-54)**

David was angry — angry at God! And he was afraid of God also, thinking, "How can the Ark of the LORD ever come to me?" (2 Samuel 6:9). David had the Ark taken to a nearby home, the home of Obed-Edom.

A parallel passage, 1 Chronicles 15:11-15, gives us some added information to this story that is crucial to understanding the outcome. After Uzzah's death, David began to do his homework to find out the proper way to transport the Ark. After he had made his conclusions, he told the Levites, "It was because you, the Levites, did not bring it up the first time that the LORD our God broke out in anger against us. WE DID NOT INQUIRE OF HIM ABOUT HOW TO DO IT IN THE PRESCRIBED WAY."

David repented!!! His sensitive heart almost broke at seeing the death of Uzzah. But, he knew something had to be wrong. He had not inquired of the Lord. This entire situation could have been solved ahead of time if he had only asked God how He wanted it to be done. I wonder how many of the defeats that we experience in this life are simply a result of not inquiring of the Lord.

So, three months later, after hearing that Obed-Edom had been blessed greatly, David decided to bring the Ark to Jerusalem. This time it would be brought God's way. "When those who were carrying the ark of the LORD had taken six steps, he sacrificed a bull and a fattened calf. David, wearing a linen ephod, danced before the LORD with all his might, while he and the entire house of Israel brought up the Ark of the LORD with shouts and the sound of trumpets" (2 Samuel 6:13-15). At this time in his life David probably wrote Psalm 132. This is what he had to say, "I will not enter my house or go to my bed — I will allow no sleep to my eyes, no slumber to my eyelids, till I find a place for the LORD, a dwelling for the Mighty One of Jacob."

After the Ark had been set in its place, David sacrificed burnt offerings and fellowship offerings before the Lord. After the sacrifices, he blessed the people in the name of the Lord Almighty. Then, he gave everyone present a loaf of bread, a cake of dates, and a cake of raisins. And all the people went home.

When David came into his own home to bless his household he was greeted by stern remarks from Michal. You see, she had seen how he had danced in the sight of the slave girls, and she thought that these actions were not fit for a king. David replied, "It was before the LORD . . . I will celebrate before the LORD" (2 Samuel 6:21). Remember: David had only ONE AUDIENCE! Michal never bore David any children, the worst curse an Israelite woman could bear.

IN CONCLUSION

Chuck Swindoll has these thoughts for us to ponder when we try to relate to the lesson that David learned in bringing the Ark into Jerusalem:

When it comes to obeying God, it's the details — the rings and poles — that snag us. Either we don't want to go to the trouble of getting the poles, or we don't want to carry them upon our shoulders. So we grab a cart, rewrite the rules, and do it our own way.

When you disobey God's precepts, He may not strike you dead like He did Uzzah, but His grief runs just as deep. Are there some rings and poles you've been ignoring? Claiming every source of income at tax time . . . being kind to someone else's difficult child . . . honoring the authorities in your life? Being a person after God's heart means caring about what He cares about, grieving over what grieves Him, and being willing to do His will, His way! (*Swindoll, p. 86*).

Read for the next lesson: 2 Samuel 7–8.

LESSON FIFTEEN

2 Samuel 7–8

GOD'S PROMISE TO DAVID

DAVID'S DREAM

With his kingdom established and all of his enemies subdued, and with the Ark of the Covenant safely within the city of Jerusalem, David had a dream. He shared this dream with the prophet, Nathan, when he said, "Here I am, living in a palace of cedar, while the ark of God remains in a tent" (2 Samuel 7:2). Nathan responded with immediate encouragement saying, "Whatever you have in mind, go ahead and do it, for the LORD is with you" (2 Samuel 7:3).

Do you see what is in David's mind? He was now living in a beautiful palace. His country was at peace. Most of the people lived in their own homes. But God still lived in a tent! What did this say to the people? Did they have their priorities right? Were they thinking of their own pleasures without even considering God? David wanted to make the worship of the One True God the number one priority of the nation. He wanted to show honor and reverence for God, the true King of Israel. So, it seemed fitting for him to build a Temple for the Lord which would display God's greatness to the entire world.

It seems that Nathan's response to David must have been a bit hasty, perhaps even too human for a prophet. You see, the Lord appeared to Nathan that same night with a message to be given to David. He had to go into the king on the next day and tell him that the excitement of the prior day was not the Lord's will. God did not want David to build Him a Temple.

With great care and genuine compassion the Lord gave Nathan a lengthy message for David. He understood that David's intentions and motives were pure, so He responded with words which are some of the most tender to be found anywhere in Scripture.

First, the Lord wanted David to see that since the days of the wilderness wanderings He had never asked any of Israel's leaders to build Him a house. Next He reminded David of how He had brought him from the fields to shepherd His people, Israel. And how He had been with him wherever he had gone. He would make David's name to become great, and plant His people so that they would no longer be disturbed.

Then God got much more personal with David. He told him that He would in fact build a house for David. He assured David that, after his death, his offspring would be king. And that the Temple that he wanted to build would, in fact, be built by his own son, a man of peace, whereas David had been a man of war (see 1 Chronicles 22:8). He explained that He would never take His love from David's son, as He took it away from Saul. Finally, the Lord said, "Your house and your kingdom will endure forever before me; your throne will be established forever" (2 Samuel 7:16).

God had said "no" to David's request to build the Temple; instead He said, "I will build a house for you." David offered to do something for God; instead, God showed His majesty and what He planned to do for David. David proposed an earthly structure; instead, God promised a never-ending kingdom that could only be seen by faith. This promise was gloriously fulfilled in David's descendant, Jesus Christ, our everlasting king (see Luke 1:32).

DAVID'S RESPONSE TO GOD'S PROMISE

David had a sensitive enough heart so that he didn't feel put down by Nathan's message of denial. You see, God had brought David far beyond his own expectations. So, David went before the Lord, quietly, humbly, probably on his knees, and offered up one of the most eloquent and moving prayers recorded in all of Scripture. He said,

> Who am I, O Sovereign LORD, and what is my family, that you have brought me this far? And as if this were not enough in your sight, O Sovereign LORD, you have also spoken about the future of the house of your servant. Is this your usual way of dealing with man, O Sovereign LORD?
>
> What more can David say to you? For you know your servant, O Sovereign LORD. For the sake of your word and according to your will, you have done this great thing and made it known to your servant.
>
> How great you are, O Sovereign LORD! There is no one like you, and there is no God but you, as we have heard with our own ears. And who is like your people Israel — the one nation on earth that God went out to make a name for himself, and to perform great and awesome wonders by driving out nations and their gods from before your people, whom you redeemed from Egypt? You have established your people Israel as your very own forever, and you, O LORD, have become their God.
>
> And now, Lord God, keep forever the promise you have made concerning your servant and his house. Do as you promised, so that your name will be great forever. Then men will say, "The LORD Almighty is God over Israel!" And the house of your servant David will be established before you.
>
> O LORD Almighty, God of Israel, you have revealed this to your servant, saying, "I will build a house for you." So your servant has found courage to offer you this prayer. O Sovereign Lord, you are God! Your words are trustworthy, and you have given this good promise to your servant. Now be pleased to bless the house of your servant, that it may continue forever in your sight; for you, O Sovereign LORD, have spoken, and with your blessing the house of your servant will be blessed forever (2 Samuel 7:18-29).

David realized that God's "no" was not a rejection, but a redirection. He realized that when God says "no" He has a better way. He realized that the results depend "on whether at the moment when God has said 'No' you *sulk or you seek* — if you seek, you will find that God is right there with blessing such as you have never experienced before" (*Redpath, p. 171*).

From David's first words, "Who am I?", you can see that his attitude was bathed in humility. He realized that he had not deserved God's grace. He was not the main actor on this stage. It was God's stage, and David knew that he was fortunate to have spent even a moment on it with the Almighty.

> ***"This is the ultimate answer each of us, who long to know and love God, must find. It is not who I am that matters half as much as WHOSE I am."***
> **(Keller, vol. 2, p. 65)**

This was not the end of the story for David in regard to the building of the Temple. You see, God gave him the plans for the Temple and gave him the privilege of collecting all of the materials so that when Solomon began the construction years later, the plans and materials were ready to the last detail.

DAVID'S CONQUESTS

David was an incredible military leader. Men would gladly risk their lives for him on a daily basis. Over time, David's kingdom grew to be about ten times larger than when he became king. Let's see briefly how he did it.

PHILISTIA — The text simply tells us that David defeated the Philistines and subdued them. It also mentions the defeat of Metheg Ammah, which was the city of Gath, the Philistines' strongest fortified city.

MOAB — The Moabites were to the east of Israel. Their origin was in Abraham's nephew, Lot. But they had become wicked and utterly corrupt. David's own great-grandmother was from Moab. It was here that David had decided to hide his parents from an angry Saul (1 Samuel 22:3,4). Tradition has it that his parents were murdered while they lived in Moab. Perhaps this suggests why he was particularly severe with the Moabites, where he killed two-thirds of the population.

ARAM (SYRIA) — First David defeated Hadadezer, king of Zobah. He captured a thousand of his chariots, seven thousand charioteers and twenty thousand foot soldiers. He hamstrung all but a hundred of the chariot horses. This was done because the Lord forbade Israel from amassing horses and chariots for herself. He wanted them to depend on His strength. David understood this, as Psalm 20:7 proves, "Some trust in chariots and some in horses, but we trust in the name of the Lord our God." Next, the Arameans of Damascus came to help Hadadezer. David struck down twenty thousand of them and set up garrisons throughout the land.

HAMATH — When Tou, king of Hamath, heard of David's great victories over Syria he sent his own son, Joram, along with articles of silver and gold, to congratulate David and to establish a treaty with David.

EDOM — While battling Edom, David's army struck down eighteen thousand Edomites in the Valley of Salt. He set up garrisons throughout the land and all the Edomites became subject to David.

Notice the significance of David's victories. He had defeated all the nations to the north, south, east, and west of Israel. He also had gained the land that God had promised originally to Abraham back in the book of Genesis.

In genuine gratitude to God for all His blessings, David chose to dedicate to the Lord most of the rare and beautiful treasures that he had aquired from those that he conquered. He clearly recognized that all possessions and the ability to gain wealth were granted to him by the generosity of God Himself. So, he was glad and eager to return most of it to the Giver.

Chapter eight ends with these words, "The LORD gave David victory everywhere he went."

IN CONCLUSION

So, think back to the kind of David that we saw in this lesson. We saw a man who was completely sold out to God. Even when receiving the big "no" from God, David could rejoice. His humble spirit led him to his knees in gratitude for what God had done in his life. How about you? How do you handle the disappointments in life? Do you *sulk*, or do you *seek* the Lord to find out what he has in store for you? Turn to Him, and receive His bountiful blessings.

LESSON SIXTEEN

2 Samuel 9–10

DAVID'S KINDNESS TO MEPHIBOSHETH

David was now at the high point of his career. Not only was he the king of Israel, but he had subdued all of the nations around him. In fact, this was the first time that Israel actually possessed all of the land that God had promised Abraham way back in the book of Genesis. It probably took somewhere around twenty years to accomplish all of this, so we're looking at a man who was now approximately fifty years old.

As the undisputed king over the entire region, David now had time to reflect and rest awhile. One day, while thinking of days long gone by, David said, "Is there anyone still left of the house of Saul to whom I can show kindness for Jonathan's sake?" (2 Samuel 9:1). You might remember that David and Jonathan had made a covenant with one another where David had promised that he would never "cut off his kindness" from the family of Jonathan (1 Samuel 20:12-19). Notice also that David's question is unconditional in regards to who the person might be. He was looking for "anyone" that he could show kindness to.

To find the answer to David's question, a servant of Saul's household, Ziba, was brought in. He told the king about a son of Jonathan, Mephibosheth, who was crippled in both feet. So David sent for him at once.

The question arises immediately as to where Mephibosheth had been all these years and why David hadn't ever heard about him before. Well, the story of Mephibosheth goes way back about twenty years. When the news of Saul and Jonathan's death reached Saul's household, Mephibosheth was five years old. At hearing such terrible news his nurse picked him up to flee. In her haste, she dropped the small lad and he became crippled. She may have been concerned that the Philistines were going to come and destroy the entire household of Saul. Or, she may have realized that Mephibosheth, being Jonathan's son, was heir to the throne after the death of his grandfather and father. She may have even fled to hide him from David, who was known to all to have been promised the throne by God Himself.

It is also interesting to note that he was living in the town of Lo Debar. Lo Debar means "no pasture." It was in Gilead, east of the Jordan. So we find the son of Jonathan living in a barren land, a land of nothingness, apparently hiding from the king.

Mephibosheth came peacefully to see the king. But you can imagine what must have been going through his mind. You see, it was very common for ancient rulers to initiate such a search. Most wanted to kill members of the previous ruling family who might one day challenge their reigns. As Mephibosheth came in to see David he bowed down to pay him honor (I think that Mephibosheth thought that his head may be cut off right on the spot — as he had heard stories of other men who were so quickly dealt with by David). But David had a different purpose in mind.

"David said, 'Mephibosheth!' 'Your servant,' he replied. 'Don't be afraid,' David said to him, 'for I will surely show you kindness for the sake of your father Jonathan. I will restore to you all the land that belonged to your grandfather Saul, and you will always eat at my table' " (2 Samuel 9:6,7).

In true humility Mephibosheth bowed down and said, "What is your servant, that you should notice a dead dog like me?" Doesn't this sound like David in our last lesson? When God gave him such great promises of what the future would bring, David said, "Who am I?" Neither David nor Mephibosheth became aggressive and demanding when speaking with someone who was an authority over them. Each humbly accepted the graces bestowed upon them. Oh, how this is so different than what we see today, with so many different people, and groups of people, demanding what they call their "rights" from those who have authority over them. We have a lot to learn from David and Mephibosheth.

Then David had Ziba brought back in. David explained that he had given Mephibosheth everything that had belonged to his grandfather, Saul. And, Ziba and his household were to farm the land so that Mephibosheth's needs would all be met. In addition, David explained that Mephibosheth would eat at David's table on a daily basis.

Mephibosheth was overwhelmed! He was hiding, now he would eat at the king's table. He owned nothing, now he was rich, with at least thirty-five servants. He considered himself a "dead dog," but David had symbolically adopted him into the royal household.

> ***"This is precisely the picture of the even greater generosity of our Most High King. It is He who comes to seek us, to find us, to pick us up in our poverty and despair. It is He who in loving kindness and tender mercy extends to us His love. He invites us to share the bounties of His household. He bestows on us the honor to be His sons and daughters!"***
> **(Keller, vol. 2, p. 76)**

DAVID DEFEATS THE AMMONITES

Up to this point in the reign of David we have heard no details about any wars with the Ammonites, located to the east of Israel. 2 Samuel 8:12 simply mentions them along with other nations that David had subdued. Perhaps they enjoyed a peaceful treaty with David, because when Nahash, the king of Ammon, died, he said, "I will show kindness to Hanun son of Nahash, just as his father showed kindness to me" (2 Samuel 10:2).

David sent a delegation of men to express his sympathy to Hanun. However, Hanun's advisors thought that David was up to something and that these men were spies. So, "Hanun seized David's men, shaved off half of each man's beard, cut off their garments in the middle at the buttocks and sent them away" (2 Samuel 10:4). These actions were seen by all in that day as a terrible disgrace to David's men.

David was enraged! He told the delegation to stay at Jericho until their beards had grown back. Then, he sent Joab out with the entire army of fighting men, to avenge the actions of Hanun. Meanwhile, Hanun had hired twenty thousand soldiers from Beth Rehob and Zobah (Arameans who were already subject to David), one thousand from Maacah, and twelve thousand from Tob.

When Joab arrived he realized that there were battle lines in front and in back of him. He took the best men and led them against the Arameans. The other men were led by his brother, Abishai, against the Ammonites. They agreed that if one group proved too powerful for them, that they would help support one another. Then the ruthless Joab stated these words, "Be strong and let us fight bravely for our people and the cities of our God. The LORD will do what is good in his sight" (2 Samuel 10:12). Rarely had Joab showed signs of true faith, but under these obstacles he simply handed the situation over to the Lord.

The Arameans fled before Joab and his forces. When the Ammonites saw this, they fled before Abishai and his forces. So, Israel had yet another victory. However, the Arameans were not done fighting. Not only did they regroup, but they sent for more soldiers from beyond the Euphrates River. When David heard this, he himself led the entire nation into war, soundly defeating Aram and her allies, who all made peace with the Israelites and became subject to them. The Arameans finally learned their lesson, as the text says, "So the Arameans were afraid to help the Ammonites anymore" (2 Samuel 10:19).

IN CONCLUSION

The story of David and Mephibosheth gives us a great picture of God's love and grace for each of us today. See Chuck Swindoll's fine book, *David —A Man After God's Own Heart,* which lists (p. 98) "a priceless set of analogies between the crippled Mephibosheth and the king, analogies that exemplify the relationship between the sinner and the Lord."

David showed kindness to Mephibosheth. This kindness is a picture of God's kindness to us shown through His Son, Jesus Christ, but the question we need to ask is, "Who do I need to show kindness to today?" Think about it. Is it possible for others to see the love of God through us? The more you think about it, the more convinced you will be that we Christians are one of God's primary ways of showing His love for individuals here on earth. If we don't love them, who will?

Look up the following Bible passages and summarize what they teach about the disadvantaged.

✐ Leviticus 14:19-23 —

✐ Deuteronomy 15:1-11 —

✐ Matthew 19:16-30 —

✐ Luke 14:7-24 —

✐ Luke 19:1-10 —

✐ James 2:1-6 —

So, who will be the beneficiary of your love today? Tomorrow? Throughout the weeks, months, and years ahead?

Read for the next lesson: 2 Samuel 11:1–12:12.

LESSON SEVENTEEN

2 Samuel 11:1–12:12

DAVID'S SIN WITH BATHSHEBA

You'll remember that at the first of the last lesson we spoke of David being in the peak of his career. He had basically subdued all of the nations around him, and was at peace. These were the conditions which enabled him to show kindness to Mephibosheth, son of Jonathan. But, in this lesson these conditions lead David into such sin that his life would never be the same again. For, you see, 2 Samuel 11 begins with these words, "In the spring, AT THE TIME WHEN KINGS GO OFF TO WAR, David sent Joab out with the king's men and the whole Israelite army [emphasis added]." It's very clear where David was supposed to be — out in the fields with his men. But, instead, he chose to stay behind in Jerusalem and enjoy life for a change. So, here we have the king of Israel, ruler of the entire area, smug and confident, with time on his hands to burn.

> ***"If you think you are standing firm, be careful that you don't fall!"***
> **(1 Corinthians 10:12)**

✐ Before we get into the details of this story, please use the space below to make a list of things that God has done for you (from simple things like providing the air you breathe to more complex things such as our redemption through Christ):

DAVID GIVES IN TO TEMPTATION

One evening David was walking around on the roof of his palace when he saw a beautiful woman bathing. Instead of running away from this temptation, as Joseph had done (Genesis 39), David enjoyed the sensuous scene. His lust became fully ablaze. He was not simply happy to have such a sight, NO!, he wanted to know who she was. He was told that she was Bathsheba, the daughter of Eliam and the wife of Uriah the Hittite. These men were numbered among David's "mighty men" (2 Samuel 23:34,39). David's thoughts should have ceased immediately. But NO! His contemplation had gone too far (or so he thought). He wanted this woman. (By the way, David had many wives and concubines of his own). Like a runaway train, David in lust commanded that she be brought to him. She came to him and he slept with her. Apparently, David thought that this was a "one night stand," until Bathsheba sent word to him that she was pregnant. David would now reap the sin that he had sown.

Today we hear from all around us, "It's OK if it's two consenting adults who are not hurting anyone." Well, that is why Scripture is so clear to "Flee fornication" (1 Corinthians 6:18), and "youthful lusts" (2 Timothy 2:22). For, as we'll see from this story, everyone involved is ultimately hurt.

One question that may arise at this time is the involvement of Bathsheba in this incident. Some believe that she deliberately seduced David. However, she is never mentioned in Scripture as the guilty party. But she does have some responsibility in the matter. After all, it was her nakedness which led to David's sin. Women, your clothing, or the lack thereof, can be a great temptation to the men around you. Conduct yourself in modesty and purity!

WHAT TO DO WITH BATHSHEBA'S HUSBAND

David had himself in a real quandary. What was he to do? Finally he devised a plan. The king invited the soldier, Uriah, to come home for a period of rest. David hoped that Uriah would go to his home, have relations with his wife, and then assume that the child which she would bear was his own. However, Uriah failed to cooperate. As a soldier he felt that it was inappropriate for him to enjoy the luxuries of home when he should be in the fields with the other men. So that night David got him drunk, thinking that he would for sure go home to his wife, if even in a stupor. No way! URIAH DRUNK WAS A BETTER MAN THAN DAVID SOBER!

So, David sent a note back with Uriah telling Joab to place Uriah on the front lines and withdraw from him so that he would be killed. Joab followed orders, and finally word came back to David of Uriah's death. After the proper time of mourning, David had Bathsheba brought to his house as his wife.

David had been a success at covering up his actions. Or had he? Perhaps the people did not know of David's deceit, but the last verse of 2 Samuel 11 says, "But the thing David had done displeased the Lord."

NATHAN CONFRONTS DAVID

In their fine book, *The Language of Love* (pp. 52-53), Gary Smalley and John Trent give an excellent paraphrase of the story. Their description of the scene ends thus:

> The large throne room had the acoustics of a Gothic Church. When the king's angry words ceased reverberating from the walls, a heavy silence fell upon the room. Ears were poised with anticipation. Though the adviser never spoke above a whisper, the impact of his words crashed through the room like peals of thunder.
>
> "Your Majesty," he began, "YOU are that man! The little lamb you took was another man's wife!"

Nathan continued, "This is what the LORD, the God of Israel, says: 'I anointed you king over Israel, and I delivered you from the hand of Saul. I gave your master's house to you, and your master's wives into your arms. I gave you the house of Israel and Judah. And if all this had been too little, I would have given you even more. Why did you *despise the word of the LORD* by doing what is evil in his eyes? You struck down Uriah the Hittite with the sword and took his wife to be your own. You killed him with the sword of the Ammonites. Now, therefore, the sword will never depart from your house, because *you despised me* and took the wife of Uriah the Hittite to be your own" (2 Samuel 12:7-9, emphasis added).

FEELING REBELLIOUS?

There are those times in each of our lives when we feel rebellious. For some ridiculous reason we think that we are wiser than God. Granted, these times usually come when Satan has his chains of forgetfulness wrapped around us. In this passage the Lord gives us two questions to ask ourselves when we feel that sense of rebellion creeping into our lives.

#1 WHAT HAS THE LORD DONE FOR YOU? God's first message to David after Nathan had said, "You are the man," was to remind him of all the wonderful things that He had done for David. "I anointed you king, . . . delivered you from Saul, . . . gave your master's house and wives to you, . . . gave you the house of Israel and Judah, . . . and if this had been too little, I would have given you even more." What has the Lord done for you? Take a look back at page 72. If you haven't already done so, make a list of the wonderful things that the Lord has done for you. And the next time you're feeling rebellious, remember what He has done for you. It will put life back into its proper perspective again.

#2 DO YOU DESPISE GOD'S WORD, AND GOD HIMSELF? Did you see this as you read through the story? God actually told David that he had despised His Word (v. 9), and even God Himself (v. 10). David, of all people, despise God's Word? Isn't that a bit strong? Listen, when we sin, we despise the Word of the Lord because, knowing what God says, we choose to do what we want. It is out-and-out rebellion! Having despised God's Word leads us to despise God Himself. What we are really saying is, "I'm going to do my own thing because I prefer me to God." Do you despise God? Of course not! So, the next time you're feeling a bit rebellious, ask yourself if you are willing through your actions to tell God that you despise Him. I think it will have a bearing on your decision.

CONCLUSION

Can what happened to David happen to us? For one whose conscience bothered him for cutting off a tiny piece of Saul's robe, something had changed. Perhaps his wealth, prosperity, and ease made him careless. Were his quiet times with God less frequent now that he wasn't hiding in places like caves or a lonely desert with only God for companionship? Was his dependence upon God wavering because his daily needs seemed so well met? How easy it is for us all to get careless when all is going well! "If you think you are standing firm, be careful that you don't fall!" (1 Corinthians 10:12).

Read for the next lesson: 2 Samuel 12 and Psalm 51.

LESSON EIGHTEEN

2 Samuel 12; Psalm 51

DAVID'S REPENTANCE

INTRODUCTION

In the last lesson we saw David, a man after God's own heart, caught up in a terrible sin. This lesson will help us to see even more clearly how terrible his sin actually was as we take a look at its consequences.

Each of us, if honest, has to admit that there are those times when we feel rebellious. For some reason we get some space between us and God and therefore want to try life by our own rules for awhile. In David's story, the Lord gave us some sobering thoughts to remember at these times in our lives. *First,* we are to consider what the Lord has done for us. Thinking of His Majesty and Mercy draws us back to Him. *Second,* He made us to see that acts of rebellion tell God that we despise Him. Wow! In fact, in another passage God says that, "rebellion is like the sin of divination" (1 Samuel 15:23). Divination was used in the worship of the false gods, so you can see how far we get from our goal of bringing honor to God when we have a rebellious spirit. He also gives us one more consideration through this story.

#3 HOW DO YOU FEEL WHEN SOMEONE TAKES THE LORD'S NAME IN VAIN? You see, when we sin we give the world the opportunity to laugh at our God. God told David, "By doing this you have made the enemies of the Lord show utter contempt" (2 Samuel 12:14). If they see no difference in us, they see no reason to believe in the God in whom we have put our trust. The world laughs at the hypocrisy in the Church today.

So . . . when we sin, we are; 1) forgetting the great things that God has done for us, 2) hating God's Word, 3) despising God Himself, and 4) giving carte blanche to God's enemies to justify their own behavior. Wow!!! Do not be deceived! Our sins impact everyone around us, believer and non-believer alike! But perhaps worse still is that it impacts our own heart, so that there is blockage between us and God.

You see, David had sinned and he knew it. But rather than face up to it, he chose to pretend that there was nothing wrong. He kept busy. He ran the kingdom. He made appearances. He worshiped the Lord in a public, ceremonial way. He attended the right meetings, said the right words, and gave the right answers (Does this sound at all like you?). But something was drastically wrong! We see no Psalms written during this year in David's life. On the outside, everything was right. But on the inside, David's heart cried out to be made right with God. In fact, later, when thinking back on this time in his life, David wrote, "When I kept silent, my bones wasted away through my groaning all day long. For day and night your hand was heavy upon me; my strength was sapped as in the heat of summer" (Psalm 32:3,4).

DAVID IS BROKEN

You know, it really didn't take much to break David's rebellious spirit. Nathan confronted the king with his sin (see the last lesson). A simple story of a poor family's lamb being stolen by a rich man and David's terrible sin is suddenly staring him in the face. David's defenses crumbled as he fell on his knees in confession and repentance.

An incredible thing happened after David's confession. The Lord gave David a Psalm — the type of Psalm that has proven to be an encouragement to millions that have found themselves caught in sin. Let's take a look:

PSALM 51

1 Have mercy on me, O God, according to your unfailing love;
according to your great compassion blot out my transgressions.
2 Wash away all my iniquity and cleanse me from my sin.

3 For I know my transgressions, and my sin is always before me.
4 Against you, you only, have I sinned and done what is evil in your sight,
so that you are proved right when you speak and justified when you judge.
5 Surely I have been a sinner from birth,
sinful from the time my mother conceived me.
6 Surely you desire truth in the inner parts;
you teach me wisdom in the inmost place.

7 Cleanse me with hyssop, and I will be clean;
wash me, and I will be whiter than snow.
8 Let me hear joy and gladness; let the bones you have crushed rejoice.
9 Hide your face from my sins and blot out all my iniquity.

10 Create in me a pure heart, O God, and renew a steadfast spirit within me.
11 Do not cast me from your presence or take your Holy Spirit from me.
12 Restore to me the joy of your salvation
and grant me a willing spirit, to sustain me.

13 Then I will teach transgressors your ways, and sinners will turn back to you.
14 Save me from bloodguilt, O God, the God who saves me,
and my tongue will sing of your righteousness.
15 O Lord, open my lips, and my mouth will declare your praise.
16 You do not delight in sacrifice, or I would bring it;
you do not take pleasure in burnt offerings.
17 The sacrifices of God are a broken spirit;
a broken and contrite heart, O God, you will not despise.

18 In your good pleasure make Zion prosper; build up the walls of Jerusalem.
19 Then there will be righteous sacrifices, whole burnt offerings to delight you;
then bulls will be offered on your altar.

> ***"The amazing grace of our merciful Lord is beyond human comprehension. He will pick up, restore and remake anyone who in utter sincerity casts themselves upon His mercy. His love far transcends anything known among men."* (Keller, vol. 2, p. 249)**

When we pray a prayer of confession, we can follow David's example.

1) *Pray for mercy!* David did not come before God on the basis of his own goodness — No way! He came before God based on God's character traits of mercy, grace, and compassion. He did not ask for justice. It's a good thing, too, because he would have been killed soon if God chose to grant David justice. David was unworthy, and so are we. Please remember this.

2) *David accepted responsibility for his sin.* Nowhere in this prayer do you see David blaming anyone but himself. He does not say that she was just too beautiful, or that she seduced him, or that he couldn't help himself, or any other such nonsense. He continually pointed the finger at himself, using first person terms such as: I, my, and me. Don't get caught up rationalizing away the responsibility for your sin. You chose to do it. Admit it! It can be the beginning of true freedom in your life.

3) *David had "One Audience."* We've said this before. David was preoccupied with his relationship with God. That's all that truly mattered. Here he said that his sin was against God, and Him only (v. 4). What about Bathsheba, Uriah, Eliam, the nation? His sin was against all these also. But what was of primary concern was his relationship with his God. That's what would last for all eternity.

4) *David knew that only God could completely cleanse him.* David alone could not take away the guilt. He felt contaminated and filthy. He said to God, "Cleanse me . . , wash me . . , blot out all my iniquity . . , create in me a pure heart . . , and restore to me the joy of your salvation." David saw himself as despicable in God's sight, and saw that his only hope was to have God completely forgive, clean, and create a brand new heart for him. Isn't this what God wants to hear from us — complete dependence upon His power, not our own. We please God most when we truly give our everything into His hands instead of telling Him what our hands will attempt to do for Him.

5) *David understood his responsibility to others.* Don't you suppose that for this entire period of time David had lacked in what we would call "Personal Witnessing." Oh sure, he put in his time in public worship. But the overflowing heart that would naturally speak of God's greatness to anyone who would listen was stifled. He was again accepting his responsibility to others by saying, "Then I will teach transgressors your ways . . , my tongue will speak of your righteousness . . , and my mouth will declare your praise."

Do we know for sure that God forgave David? Oh, yes, for listen to David's own words on this subject:

Blessed is he
  whose transgressions are forgiven,
  whose sins are covered.
Blessed is the man
  whose sin the LORD does not count against him
  and in whose spirit is no deceit.

I said, "I will confess
  my transgressions to the LORD" —
and you forgave
  the guilt of my sin.

Psalm 32:1, 2, and 5

WHAT ABOUT FORGIVENESS?

Read the following passages and come to your own conclusions concerning the completeness of God's forgiveness.

Psalm 103:12 — "As far as the east is from the west, so far has he removed our transgression from us."

Isaiah 1:18 — "Though your sins are like scarlet, they shall be as white as snow; though they are red as crimson, they shall be like wool."

Micah 7:19 — "You will tread our sins underfoot and hurl all our iniquities into the depths of the sea."

Colossians 1:13,14 — "For he has rescued us from the dominion of darkness and brought us into the kingdom of the Son he loves, in whom we have redemption, the forgiveness of sins."

Hebrews 10:17 — "Their sins and lawless acts I will remember no more."

1 John 1:9 — "If we confess our sins he is faithful and just and will forgive us our sins and purify us from all unrighteousness."

> ***"God does not require a perfect, sinless life to have fellowship with Him, but He does require that we be serious about holiness, that we grieve over sin in our lives instead of justifying it, and that we earnestly pursue holiness as a way of life."* (Bridges, pp. 40–41)**

TRUTH & CONSEQUENCES

Now that the truth was out in the open we might think that David's sin was totally gone, never to interfere with his life again. Wrong! "Do not be deceived: God cannot be mocked. A man reaps what he sows" (Galatians 6:7). David's confession brought him forgiveness. But it could not change the course of events his choices had set in motion. David would not die, but the child born to David and Bathsheba would die. One day David would go to be with the son whom the Lord had taken, but that son would never know David on earth.

That's not all! The consequences included great calamity that would come upon David from within his own household. Our next few lessons will highlight this for us. God's grace, however, was never taken from David, for Bathsheba conceived again and bore a son to David. His name was Solomon. God named him Jedidiah, meaning "loved by the LORD."

Think a moment about the "Truth & Consequences" in your own life. Are you prepared to face the sin in your own life? Oh, sure we're appalled at the power of communism, but are we as appalled at the power that sin can have over our lives? God is waiting to have a rich fellowship with us, if we would only daily allow him to have complete control over our spirit, soul, mind, and body. Don't let your bones waste away — confess and accept God's best for your life!!!

Read for the next lesson: 2 Samuel 13–15.

LESSON NINETEEN

2 Samuel 13–15

DAVID REAPS THE CONSEQUENCES OF HIS SIN

INTRODUCTION

In our last few lessons we have seen how terrible the sin was that David had committed. We also took a look into our own lives to be convicted once again of the terribleness of sin in our lives. Sin is there, always with us, looking for any opportunity to bring us down. Oh, for a commitment to Christ that leads us to truly see ourselves as "dead to sin."

Even with this commitment we need to realize that the sin in our lives that does creep to the surface will still have great impact on our lives and on those around us. God does forgive us. Praise the Lord!!! But, there are still consequences which result from our sin. God told David, "Out of your own household I am going to bring calamity upon you. Before your very eyes I will take your wives and give them to one who is close to you, and he will lie with your wives in broad daylight. You did it in secret, but I will do this thing in broad daylight before all Israel" (2 Samuel 12:11,12). Let's see how these prophecies came about in David's life.

LIKE FATHER, LIKE SON

Amnon, David's oldest son, fell madly in love with Tamar, one of his half-sisters. So intense was Amnon's passion for Tamar that it actually made him sick. But he couldn't figure out what to do about it. One day, however, a cousin (nice guy) came up with a plan that would bring Tamar into Amnon's arms. So he followed the plan. He pretended to be sick and asked his father to ask Tamar to come and care for him. She baked him some bread, and when she came to serve it to him he sent everyone out of the house and then forcibly raped her. She tried to reason with him, saying, "Don't, my brother! Don't force me. Such a thing should not be done in Israel! Don't do this wicked thing. What about me? Where could I get rid of my disgrace? And what about you? You would be like one of the wicked fools in Israel. Please speak to the king; he will not keep me from being married to you" (2 Samuel 13:12,13). But Amnon would not listen to her, and with his superior strength, he raped her. Then he hated her even more than he had loved her.

David was furious, but what did he do about it? The Bible says nothing about any punishment to Amnon. One wonders if David felt compromised and weakened because of his own adulterous affair with Bathsheba. How could he rebuke his son for something that he had also done? This may have been David's thinking, but it is false. His eyes had to be focused on his own guilt and shame if he was thinking this way. Are those of us with children actually to think that we are not to rebuke our children when they are involved in a sin that we once were involved in? No way!!! We know now how terrible that sin was in our life. We can look back and see how it drastically affected our relationship with God and others. We can speak out of experience and help our children to learn from our mistakes.

A BROTHER'S REVENGE

Absalom, Tamar's full brother, grew to hate Amnon with a great passion. It seems that his hatred even related back to the fact that David had done nothing to Amnon, as Absalom waited two full years to get his revenge. If David had punished Amnon properly, Absalom may have never taken things into his own hands.

Absalom was having a party to celebrate his revenues during sheep shearing season. He invited his father, but David declined. So, Absalom insisted that Amnon attend. David not only sent Amnon, but he sent all of the king's sons. During the party, when Amnon was intoxicated with wine, Absalom ordered his servants to strike him down, which they did (hadn't Absalom's father used the powers of wine in his scheming against Uriah?). The king's sons hurriedly fled back to Jerusalem.

Meanwhile, Absalom had fled to his grandfather, Talmai, the king of Geshur. David, in his younger life, would have sent a delegation to find Absalom and bring him to justice. But at this point, perhaps with his memory of what he had done to Uriah still fresh on his mind, David let the situation rest. Strangely, David mourned the death of Amnon only briefly, but his heart yearned for Absalom.

ABSALOM RETURNS TO JERUSALEM

Joab became quite annoyed at David's sulking attitude regarding Absalom. So, he hired a woman to tell David a sad story in which she said she was a widow in danger of losing her only remaining son who had gotten into a fight with his brother and killed him. Her neighbors now demanded that the offending son be put to death for his crime, which would leave the poor woman without any family or support. As Joab suspected, David's heart was moved by the story. The woman then skillfully turned the story around to apply it to David's treatment of Absalom. David got the point, and agreed that Absalom could return home. Joab personally went to Geshur to bring Absalom back. When they arrived, David stated that Absalom must never see his face again. So Absalom went to his own house and did not see the face of the king. Within two years, however, Absalom once again found himself greeting the king with a kiss.

It's interesting to see how David handled this entire situation.

#1 Justice was never served in the life of Absalom — if David was going to bring him back to Jerusalem, it had to be to secure justice in the case.

#2 Why listen to this woman's story and grant her wish? The law was clear in these types of cases. It was to be "eye for eye, tooth for tooth, life for life." Did he inquire of the Lord? No! And we can remember that in his younger years if he did not inquire of the Lord, the situation always turned against him. It is still true in his older years.

#3 Why not let Absalom see his face? His pride had gotten a hold on him so that he would not totally forgive him, although it tore his heart up to do so. What was actually happening in David's life, and, for that matter, in his family and in the kingdom, was a dangerous breakdown of law and order.

> ***"Too many parents have 'tunnel vision' with respect to their own offspring. They wear 'blinders' to their misdeeds. They indulge their misconduct. This is a great evil."*** **(Keller, vol. 2, p. 251)**

ABSALOM, THE SLICK POLITICIAN

One might think that the king and his son, Absalom, lived happily ever after. But, life is not so simple. You see, Absalom detested his father and wanted his position as king. He detested the fact that David had sent Tamar into Amnon's room. He detested the fact that he had done nothing to punish Amnon. He detested David's half-hearted forgiveness towards himself. And he detested the fact that the nation seemed to be lacking a leader. On this thought he knew that he could do something.

Absalom purchased a chariot and horses and got fifty men to run ahead of him throughout the land. He would get up early and stand by the side of the road. When people would come seeking justice, he would claim that there was no representative of the king to hear the case. Then he would say, "If only I were appointed judge in the land! Then everyone who has a complaint or case could come to me and I would see that he gets justice" (2 Samuel 15:4). Scripture also tells us that in all Israel there was not a man so highly praised for his handsome appearance as Absalom, especially his beautiful hair. So, with good looks and deceitful politicking, he stole the hearts of the men of Israel. Finally, after four years of these actions, Absalom felt that his time had come.

ABSALOM REVOLTS

Absalom asked his father for permission to go to Hebron to fulfill a vow, which David allowed. But Absalom had other plans in mind. He secretly sent messengers throughout the land to announce that he was becoming king. He even got David's counselor, Ahithophel, the Gilonite, to join him in his conspiracy (it's interesting to note that Ahithophel was Bathsheba's grandfather. I wonder if he still held a grudge against David for what he had done years earlier — see 11:3 and 23:34).

When David heard the reports of Absalom's plan, and the popularity of his son, he decided to flee Jerusalem. He set out to the east with his entire household following him, but left ten concubines to take care of the palace.

The Levites had brought along the ark of the covenant, but David told the faithful priest Zadok, "Take the ark of God back into the city. If I find favor in the LORD's eyes, he will bring me back and let me see it and his dwelling place again. But if he says, 'I am not pleased with you,' then I am ready; let him do to me whatever seems good to him" (2 Samuel 15:25,26). David also asked Zadok to go back to Jerusalem and be his eyes and ears there. So, he did as the king had asked and his son, Ahimaaz, and Abiathar's son, Jonathan, would take messages back and forth between the priests and David. David also asked his friend Hushai to return to Jerusalem and attempt to frustrate the advice of Ahithophel.

As David fled the city he wept as he went, with his head covered and his feet bare. Here he stood at the very lowest of his entire career as a ruler in Israel. His own son had usurped the throne. His own people, whom he had served so well, had turned from him. His own military prowess had been eclipsed so that he was forced to flee as a fugitive from the violence of his own family. This would drive any man to tears. His tears flowed as he saw the consequences of his own sin coming down upon the entire nation. And he cried because it was his own son who would do such a thing against him. He wrote, "If an enemy were insulting me, I could endure it; if a foe were raising himself against me, I could hide from him. But it is YOU (Absalom), a man like myself, my companion, my close friend, with whom I once enjoyed sweet fellowship as we walked with the throng at the house of God" (Psalm 55:12-14).

He also wrote PSALM 3 as he fled from Absalom.

> 1O LORD, how many are my foes! How many rise up against me!
>
> 2Many are saying of me, "God will not deliver him."

3But you are a shield around me, O LORD,
my Gracious One, who lifts up my head.
4To the LORD I cry aloud, and he answers me from his holy hill.
5I lie down and sleep; I wake again, because the LORD sustains me.
6I will not fear the tens of thousands drawn up against me on every side.

7Arise, O LORD! Deliver me, O my God!
For you have struck all my enemies on the jaw;
you have broken the teeth of the wicked.
8From the LORD comes deliverance.
May your blessing be on your people.

What a frustrating time for David. In his early days, as he fled from Saul, he knew that God would rescue him. He could be confident, knowing that he was innocent. But now things are different. He is no longer innocent. And he is seeing clearly the impact of his sin on those dearest to him. Oh, how it broke his heart. But, at the same time, his confidence was still in the Lord. Earlier, while talking to Zadok the priest, he expressed his feelings that God may *not* bless him with his return to Jerusalem. That was David's wish, but more important than having his wish granted was the assurance that his God was with him all of the way. And this David never forgot, as he stated in the above Psalm that God was a Shield, his Glorious One, his Sustainer, and his Deliverer. David truly seemed to understand that God, "disciplines those he loves, and he punishes everyone he accepts as a son" (Hebrews 12:6).

No matter how tough life becomes we can be confident that God has all things in control. Perhaps we are being disciplined, or perhaps we're being tested. But, through it all we can say with David, "It is good for me to be afflicted so that I might learn your decrees" (Psalm 119:71).

Read for the next lesson: 2 Samuel 16:1–19:8.

LESSON TWENTY

2 Samuel 16:1–19:8

DAVID'S MEN DEFEAT ABSALOM

As David fled Jerusalem to the east, Ziba came to meet him. You'll remember that Ziba had been Saul's chief servant. When David took Mephibosheth into the palace as one of his own sons, Ziba was given the responsibility of caring for all of Saul's property for Mephibosheth (at Saul's death, Ziba had thought that he had come to possess all that Saul had left behind). As Ziba met David he had donkeys for the king's household to ride on, food for the men, and wine for refreshment in the desert. David accepted these generous gifts and asked the whereabouts of Mephibosheth. Ziba claimed that he had stayed behind, thinking that this was his opportunity to take back the throne for his father from David's family. Nothing could be further from the truth. The only one who saw an opportunity was Ziba. He was such a shrewd opportunist that he thought that if he treated David well, David would believe him. And it worked! David gave everything that was Mephibosheth's to Ziba, and sent him on his way. Ziba never thought that he would see David again. But in our next lesson we'll see that Ziba had to use his cunning ways to once again gain David's favor.

SHIMEI CURSES DAVID

As David approached Bahurim, a man from the tribe of Benjamin, Saul's tribe, came out and began to curse David. This man had a bitter grudge against David and his family, perhaps because he thought the kingdom should be led by someone from Saul's tribe. Perhaps he even thought that he was to be the man. Whatever the case, he walked along the hillside opposite David and yelled curses at David. As he yelled, he threw stones and dirt down on David and his men. He said, "Get out, get out, you man of blood, you scoundrel! The LORD has repaid you for all the blood you shed in the household of Saul, in whose place you have reigned. The LORD has handed the kingdom over to your son Absalom. You have come to ruin because you are a man of blood!" (2 Samuel 16:7-8).

Abishai's blood began to boil when he heard such false accusations against his great king. He asked David if he could go cut Shimei's head off. David's response shows again that he truly had just "One Audience," as he told Abishai that perhaps the Lord had asked Shimei to curse him. You see, David's eyes were on the Lord, not Shimei.

Do you remember years earlier when David was living among the Philistines to avoid Saul's relentless pursuits? Do you recall that on one occasion he and his men traveled with the Philistines to wage war with Israel, but at the last minute the Philistines rejected his help? Do you remember what he discovered when he returned to Ziklag? His city had been taken by the Amalekites, and his men even spoke of stoning him. Back on page 51 we saw that David had hit rock bottom. He had lost his position, wealth, wife, country, spiritual leader, best friend, parents, new country, city, family, possessions, and friends. But "David found strength in the LORD his God" (1 Samuel 30:6).

Some people believe that David suffered more under Absalom's revolt than back in the Ziklag events. I don't know. But what I do know is that David kept his eyes on his Lord, knowing that He alone would bring him through the trials.

> ***"We do not blame our troubles and trials on others around us. We do not blame them on Satan, as so many are taught to do. We do not blame them on cruel circumstances of our little lives. Rather we see our sufferings from our Father's noble perspective. We realize that they are the stern stuff He allows to come into our experience to conform us into His own beautiful character."* (Keller, vol. 2, p. 137)**

ABSALOM ACCEPTS HUSHAI'S ADVICE

When Absalom entered Jerusalem, Hushai was there to meet him. Hushai was David's good friend who was left behind at great risk to himself to frustrate the counsel of Ahithophel. Hushai greeted Absalom with a gracious, "Long live the king! Long live the king!" (2 Samuel 16:16). He explained to Absalom that if he was God's man, then he would serve him, just as he had served his father.

Absalom then turned to Ahithophel for advice. Ahithophel told him to lie with his father's concubines who were left behind to care for the palace. This may seem like a strange thing to begin a new kingship, but in ancient times this was one way to prove that a new monarch was now in power. So, they pitched a tent on the roof of the palace (the same roof where David first set his eyes on Bathsheba) and one by one Absalom had relations with his father's concubines. Little did Absalom know that he was directly fulfilling the prophecy of Nathan, which said, "Before your very eyes I will take your wives and give them to one who is close to you, and he will lie with your wives in broad daylight" (2 Samuel 12:11).

Ahithophel's next advice was simple — attack David at once, while he is still weary and weak. This sounded good to Absalom, but he called in Hushai for his advice also. Hushai told him that it would be far better if he could summon all the fighting men from Israel and personally lead them into battle to crush his father forever. It seems that Absalom's pride liked the picture of this, so he accepted Hushai's advice.

Hushai told Zadok and Abiathar, the priests, about Ahithophel's counsel to Absalom. Not being sure what Absalom would do, they wanted to get word to David as soon as possible to cross the Jordan to safety. The priests' sons, Jonathan and Ahimaaz, took the message to David, with the help of those still loyal to David. So David and all those with him crossed the Jordan.

When Ahithophel saw that his advice had not been followed, he felt personally devastated. He felt that his dignity had been destroyed, so he saddled his donkey, traveled to his hometown, put his things in order, and hanged himself. Notice the difference between David and Ahithophel. David had been chased right off of his throne, but he humbly placed his dependence upon God to save him. On the other hand, Ahithophel, allowing his pride to control his actions went out and committed suicide — how sad! How do you handle the defeats in life? There are plenty of them, aren't there? If nothing else has been accomplished through the study of the life of David, it is my prayer that you understand that the trials in our lives are there for a purpose. They truly help us to put on the character traits of Christ.

Meanwhile, David made his home in Mahanaim, under the gracious hospitality of Barzillai, the Gileadite.

DAVID'S BATTLE WITH ABSALOM

David split his men into three troops, led by Joab, Abishai, and Ittai, the Gittite. Then he told his troops that he would even join them in the battle. They responded by convincing David that he was worth ten thousand of them and would be better off in the city. As the troops marched out, he made it clear to all that they were to be gentle with Absalom, for David's sake.

The report of the battle is quite simple. It says, "The army marched into the field to fight Israel, and the battle took place in the forest of Ephraim. There the army of Israel was defeated by David's men, and the casualties that day were great — twenty thousand men. The battle spread out over the whole countryside, and the forest claimed more lives that day than the sword" (2 Samuel 18:6-8).

Absalom himself had come out to fight in the battle. He was so confident that he didn't even wear a helmet, or any armor. Could it be that he believed the talk of his father being so weak and having no chance against his younger son? Was he so arrogant that he forgot the successes of his father in the past? In his lack of combat experience was he naive enough to think that he was not putting himself in danger? Perhaps he thought that he would simply march out with his troops to see the great defeat of his father. Wow! What a fool. While he was riding his mule, suddenly he came upon David's men. His mule took off quickly, and as it went under the thick branches of a large oak tree, Absalom's long hair got caught. He was left hanging in midair, as the mule rode away.

One of David's men spotted Absalom hanging from the tree, and since he had heard David's charge concerning Absalom, he would not do a thing to harm him. Instead, he found Joab and told him of Absalom's situation. Joab seemed surprised that the man had not killed Absalom, but this soldier said that he would never do such a thing, no matter how much Joab paid him. But Joab would wait no longer. He took three javelins and plunged them into Absalom's heart while he still hung from the tree. Then Joab sounded the trumpet. His men stopped pursuing Israel. They took Absalom, threw him into a big pit and piled a heap of rocks over him.

Why would Joab so quickly refuse to obey the words of the king? Why would he blatantly disobey his monarch? There may have been a few negative things in the past for Joab to remember — like when Absalom burned his fields, or the fact the he personally brought Absalom back to Jerusalem, only to see him revolt against David. Yes, Joab had reasons for his dislike of Absalom at this point. But, I think these things never came into his mind. You see, Joab would always do what he thought was best for David, regardless of the circumstances. He did the one thing that he thought he had to do in his loyalty to the king. He must have been thinking, "Oh, yes, the king told me not to do this, but I must, in order to preserve his throne." Can you imagine the bloody civil war that would have continued if Joab had not done this? He was a brutal man who would do anything in his support for the king. While David waited on God to act, Joab just acted.

DAVID MOURNS FOR ABSALOM

Ahimaaz, the fleet-footed one, son of Zadok, asked permission to take the news to David, back in Mahanaim. Joab declined his offer, saying that he would take the news another day, that today the news would be carried by another man. He found a Cushite, and told him to go tell David would he had seen. The man bowed before Joab in respect and then ran off. Meanwhile, Ahimaaz still wanted to be the messenger. After prodding Joab, Joab finally allowed him to also run with the news. It seems that Joab thought David might be upset by the news and he didn't want Ahimaaz, such a bright young man, to get caught in the middle of David's wrath.

Ahimaaz then outran the Cushite and shared what he thought to be good news with the king. But David wanted to know how Absalom was. Ahimaaz didn't seem to have the answer to that question. About that time the Cushite arrived with a fuller picture of the battle. Concerning Absalom, he told David, "May the enemies of my lord the king and all who rise up to harm you be like that young man" (2 Samuel 18:32).

David was crushed! He went up into the room over the gateway to the city and began to weep. He cried, "O my son Absalom! My son, my son Absalom! If only I had died instead of you — O Absalom, my son, my son!" (2 Samuel 18:33).

In his sorrow, David seemed to forget that many that day had lost their lives for him. He was burying himself in his own little pity party. But this would not last long, for Joab heard about it. Remember, Joab always did what he thought was best for his king. This time he thought it was rebuke. He told David that if he did not get out with the troops and encourage them for their loyalty and bravery, by morning not a one would still be left with him. And rebuke was exactly what David needed, for he got up and went down to the gateway of the city, where he encouraged his men.

This lesson makes it painfully clear that we do reap what we sow. David was still reaping for his sin with Bathsheba. Absalom reaped the wrath for his sins. And Joab will reap the consequences of his sin after David's death. God's Word always holds true! We will reap the consequences of our sin!!!

Read for the next lesson: 2 Samuel 19:9–20:26.

LESSON TWENTY-ONE

2 Samuel 19:9–20:26

DAVID RETURNS TO JERUSALEM

Absalom was defeated. The rebellion was over. The way was now clear for David to move back into Jerusalem. Or was it? You see, David realized that it was not wise to quickly move back into the palace. He wanted the confidence of the entire nation before he would move back. It's interesting to note that the tribes of Israel to the north were the first to want David brought back to Jerusalem. It was Judah, David's own tribe, in the south, who held out against him. He sent a message to the elders of Judah through Zadok and Abiathar, the priests. He said, "Why should you be the last to bring the king back to his palace, since what is being said throughout Israel has reached the king at his quarters? You are my brothers, my own flesh and blood. So why should you be the last to bring back the king?" (2 Samuel 19:11,12). He also sent a message to Amasa, saying, "Are you not my own flesh and blood? May God deal with me, be it ever so severely, if from now on you are not the commander of my army in place of Joab" (2 Samuel 19:13).

David had always had trouble handling Joab. We're not told how or when, but we can assume that David found out that it was Joab himself who had killed Absalom. To demote Joab because of his acts, and to lift up the tribe of Judah, David had Amasa, Absalom's general, placed in command of the army.

In this way David "won over the hearts of all the men of Judah as though they were one man" (2 Samuel 19:14). They sent word to David to come back and be their king. As David traveled back to Jerusalem he was met by many different people. Let's take a look:

SHIMEI MEETS DAVID

You'll remember that back in chapter sixteen this Benjamite, Shimei, hurled down rocks and curses on David as he fled Jerusalem. At that time Abishai wanted to go and kill Shimei for David, but David would not allow him to do so, thinking that perhaps these curses were from God Himself.

Can you imagine Shimei's response when he heard that Absalom's army had been defeated by David's. It was not too many days earlier that he thought that he had gotten away with cursing the king. He no doubt still felt that a man of Benjamin, Saul's tribe, should sit on the throne. His cursings of David probably made him feel proud that he had stood up for Saul's tribe. But, how would he feel now that David was coming back to sit on the throne of Israel? Wow! Think for a minute of the implications. Here's a man who had to run and hide, or face the man that he had cursed not long before. He decided to face David like a man.

As he met David he fell prostrate before the king and pleaded for forgiveness. Abishai still wanted to kill him, but David would not allow it. Instead he gave his word that Shimei would not die. However, he would not forget, and on his deathbed he told his son Solomon to bring Shimei's gray head down to the grave in blood.

Along with Shimei came Ziba, that shrewd servant of Saul. Like Shimei, he never dreamed David would be back. When David had fled Jerusalem, Ziba had lied to him about Mephibosheth, saying that Mephibosheth stayed in Jerusalem thinking that the kingdom would soon be his. Nothing was farther from the truth. But, being the shrewd man that he was, he was here to greet David as he came across the Jordan River, hoping to keep the king's support. It's interesting to note that David still believed Ziba to a degree. But when he saw him with Shimei it seems that David would have seen right through his deception. It even makes me wonder why a man like Ziba, looking for the king's favor, would even be seen with such a man as Shimei. These two men had a lot in common. Their shrewd dealings in the past had brought them much power among the men of Benjamin. Perhaps that's why we see them coming to David with a thousand Benjamites for support.

MEPHIBOSHETH MEETS DAVID

Mephibosheth, longing for the king's return to Jerusalem, had not taken good care of himself in the king's absence. He was actually quite a repulsive sight. He had not cared for his lame feet, trimmed his mustache, or washed his clothing from the day the king had left until this day. He pleaded his case to David, saying that Ziba had betrayed him. As he presented his case it appears that David had put up with this situation long enough. He cut short Mephibosheth's speech, and ruled that the fields were to be divided between the two of them. Here's where Mephibosheth's appreciative heart shined forth as he said, "Let him take everything, now that my lord the king has arrived home safely" (2 Samuel 19:30). Mephibosheth loved David. Even if Ziba swindled him out of everything he had, he still had David back on the throne; that's all that mattered to him.

David appears to be so tired that he didn't care that justice be served, as long as the problem was solved. Here's the contrast between a faithful and loyal servant who only wanted the king to return to Jerusalem safely on one hand, and, on the other hand, a shrewd man who never pictured the king on the throne again. Just as today justice doesn't always prevail, both of these men walked away with an equal reward (actually Ziba came out on top because earlier he was told to care for Saul's land on Mephibosheth's account — now he owned half of what he had cared for). Although Ziba seemed to win in this situation, we can be sure that the Lord saw right through to the heart of each man and would personally judge them accordingly. We can be sure that God was proud of Mephibosheth's actions, while He detested Ziba's.

BARZILLAI SAYS "GOOD-BYE"

This was the man who had provided for David while he was in Mahanaim. What a risk it had been for him to do so, because if Absalom had defeated David, you can be sure he would have come after Barzillai for his kindness to David.

Barzillai had come to the Jordan to bid farewell to David. David offered to take him to Jerusalem to provide for him. But Barzillai didn't have many years to live, being eighty at this time, and told David that the pleasures that David could offer him would not be enjoyed at his age. Besides, he wanted to die in his own town and be buried with his father and mother. However, he would send his son, Kimham, with David to Jerusalem. Kimham would receive the same royal treatment that Mephibosheth received in the king's palace.

QUARRELING BETWEEN ISRAEL AND JUDAH

After David had crossed the Jordan River many of the men of Israel appeared to have become quite envious of the men of Judah because they had all had a part in bringing David over. Their jealousy made them even ask David why such a thing had occurred. But it was the men of Judah who answered, and said basically, "Hey, what's the problem? He's our flesh and blood. We did not eat of his provisions or take anything that is his, so get off of our case." But the men of Israel claimed that they had ten shares (tribes) in the king, and therefore had more right to bring him over the river. The argument continued until Sheba led a rebellion among the men of Israel against David. Actually this jealousy, envy, and accusations continued for two more generations until the kingdom was eventually split in two, with Judah to the south, and Israel to the north.

SHEBA'S REBELLION AGAINST DAVID

Scripture introduces us to Sheba by saying that he was a troublemaker. He evidently was a rather popular person with a large following still loyal to Saul's dynasty, as he was of the tribe of Benjamin. With all this bickering going on between the men of Judah and the men of Israel, Sheba suddenly yelled out, "We have no share in David, no part in Jesse's son! Every man to his tent, O Israel!" (2 Samuel 20:1). Now you might think, "Who's going to follow such a fool?" David had been their hero. He had strengthened the kingdom beyond their wildest dreams. But when the emotional struggle between these two groups hit its peak, all the men of Israel rallied around Sheba and deserted David. They were obviously thinking with their hearts and not their heads.

After David had returned to Jerusalem he summoned Amasa and told him to gather the troops within three days to go fight against Sheba. You can imagine Amasa's challenge of motivating troops to go fight with him when just days earlier he had led Absalom's troops against David. Well, it took him longer than David had said, so David called in Abishai, Joab's brother, and told him to take the king's men and pursue Sheba (you'll remember that Abishai was the young man who went into Saul's camp at night with David when David took Saul's spear and water jug — 1 Samuel 26).

While they were at Gibeon, Amasa came to meet them. Joab, who had been with Abishai, greeted Amasa warmly. He embraced Amasa as if to kiss him. Instead he pulled a dagger out and plunged it into Amasa's belly. This is the same way that Joab had killed Saul's general, Abner. He was a ruthless man who allowed no one to thwart his service to the king.

At seeing Amasa dead in the road, one of Joab's men yelled, "Whoever favors Joab, and whoever is for David, let him follow Joab!" (2 Samuel 20:11). It appears at this point that Joab took over the command of the troops from his younger brother, Abishai.

They finally caught up with Sheba at Abel Beth Maacah. They built a seige ramp up to the city, and as they were battering the wall a wise woman came to the wall and asked for Joab. She explained that Abel was a peaceful and faithful city, that people would come from all around Israel to Abel for sound advice. She asked why Joab was set on destroying one of the Mother cities in Israel. Joab explained that Sheba was leading a rebellion against the king and that he was held up in the city. He told her that if she would hand over this one man, the warriors would withdraw from the city.

It would be so interesting to know how she talked her fellow citizens into doing what they did next. They found Sheba, cut off his head, and threw it over the wall to Joab. He sounded the trumpet, and his men dispersed from the city, each returning to his home.

Chapter twenty of Second Samuel ends by listing David's key national leaders: "Joab was over Israel's entire army; Benaiah son of Jehoiada was over the Kerethites and Pelethites; Adoniram was in charge of the forced labor; Jehoshaphat son of Ahilud was recorder; Sheva was secretary; Zadok and Abiathar were priests; and Ira the Jairite was David's priest."

IN CONCLUSION

It's interesting to note the different ways that David dealt with the great numbers of people that he came in contact with. In each case he was to administer justice. Whether it was a respected leader of a tribe, or a simple servant, David had it in his heart to treat all properly and according to what they deserved. We must remember that this man was the most powerful man alive. He didn't have to deal with all these people, but he felt that it was his duty under God. He would respect each person, regardless of their situation in life.

Recently I heard a speaker say, "I think that the main problem in homes today is a lack of respect." And I had to agree. It seems that our kids today don't understand how to respect their elders. But then he continued, "Oh, no, I'm not talking about the kids. I don't think parents know how to respect their kids." I was caught. I was convicted. He was right. We get so caught up with our own lives, with our own pursuits, that we forget how we are to treat those around us. And yet, how we treat others says more about us than does our accomplishments.

Let's use David as our example. Or, better yet, let's use Christ as our ultimate example of one who would always consider the needs of another above his own. Let's begin to respect others as Christ does. No favoritism —just a sincere love for all that God will bring into our path.

Read for the next lesson: 2 Samuel 21–23.

LESSON TWENTY-TWO

2 Samuel 21–23

VARIOUS EVENTS IN DAVID'S LATER LIFE

THE GIBEONITES AVENGED

During David's reign as king, there was a famine in the land that lasted three years. David inquired of the Lord to see if this famine was in any way a disciplinary measure brought upon Israel by God for some sin that they had committed. The Lord answered, "It is on account of Saul and his bloodstained house; it is because he put the Gibeonites to death" (2 Samuel 21:1).

Four hundred years earlier, as Joshua led the Israelites into the land of Canaan, God powerfully moved to bring the Israelites victory against all of their enemies. The Gibeonites, however, came to Joshua and the elders and deceived them into thinking that they were from a far off land and that they wanted to make a treaty with Israel. Joshua did not inquire of the Lord and granted Gibeon this special favor. When he found out that Gibeon was within the land of Canaan, and that they were supposed to wipe them out, he concluded that they were still to keep their oath of peace with them. The Gibeonites became woodcutters and water carriers for the community and for the altar of the Lord.

Notice here the importance of keeping one's word. Joshua, as leader of Israel, made a promise to Gibeon. Years later, Saul, as leader of Israel, broke that promise. The result: three years of famine, until David resolved the situation. In our permissive society this would be considered a joke. Keeping your word is no longer a virtue in America. Climbing the ladder of success and trampling on those under you seems to carry more weight than personal integrity. How sad! And even sadder still is that this is so prevalent in our churches. I serve at a great church, but I could fill a book with stories of the times people have told me that they would do something and then they didn't come through. Folks, it is simple, for Jesus tells us, "Let your 'Yes' be 'Yes,' and your 'No,' 'No'" (Matthew 5:37).

It's your choice! Who do you want to impress? Do you want others around you to be impressed with your shrewd dealings with others, or do you want our only true *audience* in heaven to be proud of the stand you take and the values that you live by?

It's also sad to realize that we actually think that we get away with those times when we have not kept our word. This story out of Israel's history should help us to see that the results are devastating when we begin to think such nonsense.

> ***"When you make a vow to God, do not delay in fulfilling it. He has no pleasure in fools; fulfill your vow. It is better not to vow than to make a vow and not fulfill it."*** **(Ecclesiastes 5:4-5)**

Now let's get back to our story. David summoned the Gibeonites and asked them how restitution for this sin could be made. They responded that seven of Saul's male descendants should be killed and exposed before the Lord at Gibeah of Saul. David granted their request. Mephibosheth was spared because of David's covenant with Jonathan. However, seven others were handed over to the Gibeonites, who killed them and left their bodies to be exposed for everyone to see.

Rizpah, mother of two of the deceased, stayed with these bodies and would not let the birds touch them by day or the animals by night. She did this for approximately six months. When David heard of this, he sent to Jabesh Gilead for the bones of Saul and Jonathan. Then, he had these bones, plus the bones of the seven, buried in the tomb of Saul's father, Kish.

MORE WARS WITH THE PHILISTINES

It's been quite a while since we have heard anything about the Philistines. David had subdued them so well that it took them years to gain back enough strength to attempt to challenge Israel.

On one occasion David himself, probably around sixty years of age, went out with his men to fight against the Philistines. It had been years since he had done so. Physically, he was not the man that he used to be, and he became exhausted. He came up against one hulk of a man whose spearhead weighed as much as a sledge-hammer. This probably reminded him of Goliath. But things were different this time. David was about to be defeated, when Abishai, his brave nephew, came to his rescue and defeated the Philistine. His men told him, "Never again will you go out with us to battle, so that the lamp of Israel will not be extinguished" (2 Samuel 21:17).

There were other such battles with the Philistines, each won by the Israelites, and each containing stories of the defeat of giant men like Goliath.

TO GOD BE THE GLORY

Before David had ever become king, we saw the incredible difficulties that life had thrown his way. And it seems that the Lord used these times in David's life to prepare him to become the next king. But think for a moment of the difficulties that David faced as Israel's king — difficulties that would drive the average man crazy. The daily grind of administering the kingdom and expanding it to its largest size ever must have been overwhelming. Put on top of that the personal trials that David had to deal with, things such as: the death of a friend while bringing the ark of the covenant into Jerusalem, his sin with Bathsheba, his murder of Uriah, the rebellion of his son, Absalom — resulting in David's departure from the palace, and finally Absalom's death, three years of famine, and most recently the resurgence of the Philistines.

With all of these things weighing heavily on David's mind, he still did not consider blaming God for them. No! He would only bring God the glory for all of the events of his life, whether good or bad, because he knew that God was always with him to make "good" out of all "bad" circumstances.

In chapter twenty-two of 2 Samuel is recorded a psalm of David which makes it clear that his eyes were on God, to give Him the praise for all aspects of his life. Chuck Swindoll breaks this psalm into four themes (found on pages 142–144 in his fine book, *David —A Man After God's Own Heart*):

I. When Times Are Tough, the Lord Is Our Only SECURITY (2 Samuel 22:2-20)

II. When Days Are Dark, the Lord Is Our Only LIGHT (2 Samuel 22:21-31)

III. When Our Walk Is Weak, the Lord Is Our Only STRENGTH (2 Samuel 22:32-49)

IV. When Our Future Is Foggy, the Lord Is Our Only HOPE (2 Samuel 22:50-51)

A CONCLUDING THOUGHT

"We don't need to wait until the long shadows of age and pressure overtake us to stop and take a close, hard look at our lives. Are there tough times in your life? Have there been dark days? Is there a weakened walk? A foggy future? Only the Lord of security . . . light . . . strength . . . and hope can see you through. Won't you cling closely to Him during your struggles — and make David's song of triumph your own?" **(Swindoll, p. 144)**

Chapter 23 begins with what appears to be the last of the songs that came forth from David's lips. In it he still praises God, and remembers the eternal covenant that God had made with him, to make David's house to last forever.

This chapter also lists David's mighty men. Miraculous things happened when David and his men depended on God for the victory. I wonder, do you think that you would be listed on anyone's list of mighty people? Have you ministered in such a way to people that their lives would truly not be the same without you? Think about it!!!

Read for the next lesson: 2 Samuel 24.

LESSON TWENTY-THREE

2 Samuel 24

DAVID UNWISELY TAKES A CENSUS

It has often been said that "power corrupts." And in truth there are not many human beings who can handle wealth, authority, power or prominence without falling prey to its corroding pride. This includes our spiritual leaders. One big problem, however, is that when our leaders fall, they take a host of innocent people with them. Let's see how David's pride led him to a decision that resulted in the deaths of thousands of Israel's inhabitants.

DAVID ORDERS A CENSUS

In the latter years of David's reign, probably between skirmishes with the Philistines, David ordered that a census be taken of all Israel. His main concern was to know how large and powerful his standing army had become. Joab saw through David's obvious pride and questioned the king concerning his command, but David's order prevailed. For some strange reason David was putting his confidence in the strength of his army instead of the strength of his God.

> ***"Better a poor but wise youth***
> ***than an old but foolish king***
> ***who no longer knows how to take warning."***
> **(Solomon — Ecclesiastes 4:13)**

David did not inquire of the Lord, or His prophets. He simply decided to do it! In 1 Chronicles 21:1 we find out that Satan had seen this as an opportunity to tempt David. Here in 2 Samuel we see that God Himself saw these events as an opportunity to judge Israel for some unrecorded sin (24:1). We'll discuss later how God, Satan, and David all had a part in this census. At this point it is enough to say that David's power had gone to his head. He wanted to know just how powerful he had become. He wouldn't listen to anyone! He was the king, so the census would be taken.

> ***"If you find yourself in the trusted position of unquestioned authority, be careful. Life on the pedestal is precarious. When you fall from the heights, you not only fall hard, you shatter the lives of those beneath you. Don't live your life unchecked. Surround yourself with those who put integrity on a pedestal — not you."*** **(Swindoll, p. 148)**

When the census came in, David discovered that his army was made up of just under a million and a half men. Suddenly David felt conscience-stricken about the census. We do not know why he changed his mind, but he was actually heartbroken over the whole thing (doesn't this sound like the David that we want to emulate?). He said to the Lord, "I have sinned greatly in what I have done. Now, O LORD, I beg you, take away the guilt of your servant. I have done a very foolish thing" (2 Samuel 24:10).

DAVID CHOOSES HIS PUNISHMENT

The eternal consequences of sin are forever forgiven in a Christian's life, but the earthly consequences of sin, more often than not, have to be faced. The Lord sent His message to David through Gad, the prophet. You'll remember that some forty years earlier Gad had come to help David when he had hidden himself in the cave of Adullam. Instead of issuing David's punishment Himself, God allowed David to choose between three separate scenarios:

1) Three years of famine in the land,

2) Three months of fleeing from his enemies, or

3) Three days of plague in the land.

Trusting the mercy of God rather than the wrath of his enemies, David chose for three days of plague in the land. So the Lord sent a plague on Israel for three days, and seventy thousand of the people died. When the angel who was sent to carry out the Lord's punishment reached Jerusalem, the Lord was grieved and said, "Enough! Withdraw your hand" (2 Samuel 24:16).

When David saw the angel suspended in space over the city, he said to the Lord, "I am the one who has sinned and done wrong. These are but sheep. What have they done? Let your hand fall upon me and my family" (2 Samuel 24:17). David did not justify his sin. He did not blame it on someone else. He accepted responsibility for it, and asked that the burden of the punishment be directed at him and his household. Again, David was willing to see that his sin was against God; and to make it right he had to appeal to God and His mercy.

> ***"If more men and women truly saw the gravity of their sins against God, they would desist from evil. But they do not. A large portion of the responsibility for sin being so rampant in our society is that our leaders will not cry out against it. Rather, they merely protest with pious platitudes that people are 'sick,' that they 'hurt,' and what they need is soft sympathy, rather than deep heart-changing repentance."*** **(Keller, vol. 2, p. 195)**

DAVID BUILDS AN ALTAR

Throughout the recorded history of Scripture, altars have always represented a special covenant relationship between an individual and his God. Here we see Gad telling David to build an altar to the Lord on the threshing floor of Araunah, the Jebusite. As David approached Araunah, he explained that he needed his threshing floor in order to build an altar so that the plague on the people would be stopped. Araunah offered anything that David needed for free, but David would not allow it. He said, "I will not sacrifice to the Lord my God burnt offerings that cost me nothing" (2 Samuel 24:24).

So David bought the land from Araunah and built an altar. He sacrificed burnt offerings and fellowship offerings. 1 Chronicles 21:26 tells us that, "He called on the Lord, and the Lord answered him with fire from heaven on the altar of burnt offering." This fire was the visible sign by which the Lord assured David that his prayer had been heard and that his offering had been graciously accepted (see Leviticus 9:24; 1 Kings 18:38; and 2 Chronicles 7:1).

David also noticed that the angel put his sword back into its sheath, representing the end to the pestilence in Israel. The Lord ended the plague, but because of David's foolish choice, there were still seventy thousand fresh graves in Israel.

It is interesting to note that this threshing floor of Araunah was the very site on Mount Moriah where Abraham had offered his son Isaac to God, some 850 years before. And it became the spot where Solomon, David's son, would build the Temple in years to come.

SO WHO'S RESPONSIBLE FOR THE CENSUS?

The taking of this census is an interesting event because so many individuals are involved in the motivation to do so. 2 Samuel 24:1 tells us that the Lord's anger burned against Israel so He incited David to take the census. 1 Chronicles 21:1 says that Satan rose up against Israel and incited David to take the census. But it was ultimately David's decision to do so. Who's responsible? Who is to blame?

Larry Richards' fine book, *The Teacher's Commentary*, (p. 242) discusses the answer.

> The question Westerns are likely to ask is, "Who is really to blame?" We want to fix responsibility in one place, and to excuse the other actors. But the Hebrews did not view moral causation in a Western way. *The Old Testament approach to morality takes it for granted that all are responsible.* That is, God was responsible for inciting David to take the census. He had His own purpose for this action, and that purpose was a righteous one. Satan was responsible for inciting David to take the census. And Satan had *his* own purposes for taking that action. And, *David* was responsible for taking the census. He too had his own purpose in mind!
>
> In essence, each actor in this situation is viewed as both *free* and *responsible*. God incited David — but He was not responsible for David's choice. Satan incited David — but Satan was not responsible for David's choice. What God was responsible for was the act of inciting, and His reason for that act was a good, holy, and just reason. What Satan was responsible for was his act of inciting David. And Satan's reasons for his act flowed from his evil character: he was acting as the adversary and enemy of God's people. What David was responsible for was his decision to take the census. And David too had his own reasons, which commentators have suggested might have been pride, or a shifting of trust from God to military might.

Read for the next lesson: 1 Kings 1:1–2:12.

LESSON TWENTY-FOUR

1 Kings 1:1–2:12

DAVID'S FINAL CHALLENGES

PREPARATIONS FOR THE TEMPLE

It's very exciting to see how David spent his last years. He didn't retire to some mountain villa, but remained active and vibrant. His number one task became the preparations for the building of the Temple by his son, Solomon. You'll remember that David had wished to build the Temple (2 Samuel 7), but the Lord had said that David had shed too much blood to build His house. His son Solomon, a man of peace, was to be the one to do so. The Lord then promised David that He would build David's house. David was so full of gratitude and praise for the promises that God had made to him that he was not at all angry that he could not personally build the Temple. Instead, in his later years, he put his heart and his energy into making the preparations necessary for such a colossal endeavor.

In our last lesson we saw that David had bought the threshing floor of Araunah in order to build an altar so that the plague on Israel would be stopped. After the angel of God's wrath put his sword back into its sheath, Scripture records these words,

> Then David said, "*The house of the LORD God is to be here*, and also the altar of burnt offering for Israel."
>
> So David gave orders to assemble the aliens living in Israel, and from among them he appointed stonecutters to prepare dressed stone for building the house of God. He provided a large amount of iron to make nails for the doors of the gateways and for the fittings, and more bronze than could be weighed. He also provided more cedar logs than could be counted, for the Sidonians and Tyrians had brought large numbers of them to David.
>
> David said, "My son Solomon is young and inexperienced, and the house to be built for the LORD should be of *great magnificence and fame and splendor* in the sight of all the nations. Therefore, I will make preparations for it." So David made extensive preparations before his death (1 Chronicles 22:1-5, *emphasis added*).

David provided literally thousands of tons of gold and silver for the building of the Temple, along with uncounted amounts of wood, stone, and metals. He also assembled skilled workmen, and assigned individuals for each Temple duty, including musicians.

He not only made the physical preparations, but the Lord Himself gave him the exact blueprints for the Temple. It wasn't secondhand, but something David received from the Lord Himself, the plan of God's Temple which one day He would fill with His glory. This is quite like what happened in the book of Exodus, where God gave direct instructions to Moses concerning the building of the Tabernacle. "'All this is in writing,' David said, 'because the hand of the LORD was upon me, and he gave me understanding in all the details of the plan'" (1 Chronicles 28:19). Do you have an unfulfilled dream in your own life? If God has said "No," accept it and work within God's ordained will for your life. David shows us how incredible blessings are given to those who live joyously within God's will.

Yes, the plans were now completed for the building of the Temple. But, how spectacular was this great edifice? Take a look at the chart to see the great amounts of precious metals which were stored for use in the Temple. Then think what it must have looked like.

	GOLD	SILVER
COLLECTED and STORED (1 Chronicles 22:14)	3,750 TONS	37,500 TONS
DAVID'S GIFTS (1 Chronicles 29:3-5)	110 TONS	260 TONS
LEADERS' GIFTS (1 Chronicles 29:6-8)	190 TONS, 185 POUNDS	375 TONS
TOTAL	4,050 TONS, 185 POUNDS (8,100,000 POUNDS)	38,135 TONS (76,270,000 POUNDS)
WORTH IN 1991	$45 BILLION	$5 BILLION

Besides these precious metals, no exact figures are given for the incredible storehouse of bronze, iron, precious stones (onyx, turquoise), marble, rare draperies and exquisite fine furnishings that had been gathered for this magnificent building. A conservative guess would put a minimum value of at least seventy-five billion dollars worth of goods accumulated for Solomon as he began to build the Temple.

> ***"In his own rough and ready way, David was utterly convinced that the construction of a glorious temple was the highest honor he could bestow on the Lord. He was determined to actually do something beautiful for God. It was not enough for him to merely sing great psalms or compose marvelous music to the honor of his God. He longed to leave behind him — in tangible form of stone, wood, gold, silver, and precious stones — a fitting sanctuary for the Most High whom he worshiped and adored."*** **(Keller, vol. 2, p. 205)**

ADONIJAH'S CHALLENGE TO THE THRONE

As David's life came down to its last days, he became quite feeble and couldn't keep himself warm. So, his servants found a beautiful young virgin, Abishag, to care for him and to lie with him and keep him warm (however, there were never intimate relations between these two). At this time in his reign as king, it appears that he ruled as a co-regent with his son, Solomon. David had already made Solomon king in his place (1 Chronicles 23:1). It is hard to tell when this happened, but we can assume that with David limited to his quarters, no one probably burdened him with day-to-day administration of the kingdom. Solomon ruled, but not with great power as long as his father was still alive.

It appears to be during this time that Adonijah, the rightful and legitimate heir apparent to the throne, rose up to make himself the next king. He strutted around in his chariot with fifty men running ahead of him. If this sounds like Absalom, it's quite possible that both of them were raised in such a way that they would turn out to be completely spoiled, as 1 Kings 1:6 tells us that, "His father had never interfered with him by saying, 'Why do you behave as you do?'" With daily doses of discipline missing, it's no wonder that both Absalom and Adonijah grew up thinking that they could have whatever they wanted. How sad!!!

Adonijah, with the support of Joab and Abiathar, threw himself a great party; actually a coronation party.

They sacrificed many animals, ate and drank together saying, "Long live King Adonijah!"

When Nathan the prophet heard what was happening, he went to Bathsheba and told her that she must go to see the king. After she told the king the news, then Nathan was to follow her with the same news. Their plan worked quite well. David couldn't believe his ears. He called Bathsheba back in and reaffirmed the promises that he had made to her regarding Solomon.

He then called in Nathan, the prophet; Zadok, the priest; and Benaiah, the chief officer of his royal guard. He told them to

> . . . take your lord's servants with you and set Solomon my son on my own mule and take him down to Gihon. There have Zadok the priest and Nathan the prophet anoint him king over Israel. Blow the trumpet and shout, "Long live King Solomon!" Then you are to go up with him, and he is to come and sit on my throne and reign in my place. I have appointed him ruler over Israel and Judah" (1 Kings 1:33-35).

They did exactly as David had said, and while on the way back to Jerusalem, with great crowds of people rejoicing and playing the flutes so that the ground shook with the sound, Adonijah and his friends heard the commotion as they were finishing their feast. Joab seemed to be particularly annoyed. Just then, Abiathar's son, Jonathan, arrived and told them everything that had happened. At this, Adonijah's guests rose in alarm and dispersed. Adonijah was so frightened that he went to the Tabernacle and took hold of the horns of the altar, considered as a place of refuge for criminals deserving death. Here Solomon's wisdom showed itself, even at his young age, as he told Adonijah that if he proved to be a worthy man he would not be hurt, but if he proved to be evil, he would die.

DAVID'S FINAL CHARGE TO SOLOMON

When the time drew near for David to die, he gave a charge to Solomon his son:

> I am about to go the way of all the earth. So be strong, show yourself a man, and observe what the LORD your God requires: Walk in his ways, and keep his decrees and commands, his laws and requirements, as written in the Law of Moses, so that you may prosper in all you do and wherever you go, and that the LORD may keep his promise to me: "If your descendants watch how they live, and if they walk faithfully before me with all their heart and soul, you will never fail to have a man on the throne of Israel" (1 Kings 2:2–4).

David went on to tell his son to deal harshly with some men, such as Joab and Shimei. He reminded Solomon how Joab had killed Abner and Amasa, and how Shimei had thrown down curses on David like no other man ever dared to do.

Then, he told Solomon to deal kindly with the sons of Barzillai. It was Barzillai who had shown David great hospitality in Mahanaim when Absalom had dethroned him for some time. Now, his sons were to be given the same kindness that had been given to Mephibosheth, Jonathan's crippled son.

David's death was recorded with these simple words, "Then David rested with his fathers and was buried in the City of David. He had reigned forty years over Israel — seven years in Hebron and thirty-three in Jerusalem" (1 Kings 2:10-11). We are given no details of the great funeral that Israel must have provided at David's death, but 1 Chronicles 29:28 adds these words, "He died at a good old age, having enjoyed long life, wealth and honor." David began his reign at thirty (2 Samuel 5:4), thus he died at the age of seventy.

IN CONCLUSION

We have seen quite clearly throughout this study that David was not perfect. However, David lived his life with passion. He had a passion for his God. He had a passion to please his God. He had a passion to accomplish great things for his God. And he had a passion to leave behind the preparations so that God would be greatly honored in the future.

Wow!!! What an example! Now we need to honestly ask ourselves what kinds of passions keep us going in life. Are they temporal, worldly, materialistic, selfish, fleshly? Honestly, if you were to die today, what would people say was your passion in life? What were you always striving after? Now think about it, is your passion something that you can take with you when you die? David could!

We need to continually be reevaluating our values and goals in life. We need to decide if they stand up when compared to the standards set forth in Scripture. And I think it's healthy to ask ourselves what we want to leave behind for others when we leave this world.

Do you live your life with passion — a passion that others can see — a passion that is contagious? If not, why not? God is so passionate about you that He sent His Son for you. Now it's time for you to respond back in passion.

Read for the next lesson: 2 Chronicles 14–16.

LESSON TWENTY-FIVE

2 Chronicles 14–16

"HOW TO HAVE A HEART FOR GOD" ANOTHER VIEW — KING ASA

INTRODUCTION

In concluding this study on the life of David I wanted to get back to the real purpose of this study — "How to Have a Heart for God." With all the talk about what this phrase means, it seems to me that the best way to express it is still to see it come out in the life of an individual. For someone to model it for us is so much more compelling than for someone to teach its meaning to us. So, this lesson has been dedicated to this theme of having a heart for God by looking at a king who is not as well known as David. In fact, perhaps you have never even heard his name, Asa.

Asa, Solomon's great-grandson, reigned in Judah approximately sixty years after the death of David. You'll remember the tension between the tribe of Judah and the northern tribes, even throughout David's life. Well, only two generations after David, the nation of Israel split into two countries, with Judah (made up of the tribes of Judah and Benjamin) to the south and Israel (made up of the other tribes) to the north. So, we enter this story with a divided kingdom and Asa serving as king of Judah, as recorded in 2 Chronicles 14–16.

There's a verse towards the end of this passage that pretty well sums up the message of the life of king Asa. It says, "For the eyes of the LORD range throughout the earth to strengthen those whose hearts are fully committed to him" (16:9). The truth of this verse still holds true today! God's incredible strength is always there, waiting for our hearts to be fully submitted and committed to His will. It's a "cause-effect" relationship. It's an "if-then" relationship. When we do our part, fully committing our hearts to Him, it frees Him up to do mighty acts through us. And look! His eyes search for people with committed hearts. He longs to give us strength. He wants desperately to be the victorious power in our lives. But notice — the ball's in our court — we need to act! Let's see how this verse summarizes the life of king Asa.

ASA BECOMES KING

The very first verse referring to Asa says that he "did what was good and right in the eyes of the LORD" (14:2). He basically did three things to prove that he had a fully committed heart. 1) HE CLEANED UP THE SIN IN THE NATION. Scripture says that he removed all of the foreign altars and illegal places for worship, and destroyed all signs of worship to idols. 2) HE LED THE PEOPLE IN SEEKING THE LORD. And 3) HE COMMANDED THEM TO OBEY GOD'S LAWS AND COMMANDS.

The result was that Asa had peace for years. He built up the cities that no doubt were in bad shape from all the wars that had taken place over the past years. He had an army of 580,000 brave fighting men. And Asa understood the "cause-effect" relationship with God, as he stated, "The land is still ours, because we have SOUGHT HIM and he has given us rest on every side" (14:7).

> *"The Lord is with you when you are with him.*
> *If you seek him, he will be found by you,*
> *but if you forsake him, he will forsake you."* (15:2)

TEST #1

You know, it always seems to happen this way. You've finally got your life straightened out, you're doing well in most areas of your life, your relationship with God is doing fine, and it seems like you're in the middle of a period of peace, when all of a sudden the bottom falls out. All things fall apart, and you're right in the middle of it. Yes! It is a test! For Asa it was the army of Cush coming up to battle Judah. It literally says that their troops numbered a thousand thousands. This could mean a million, or it could be that the army was so big that they couldn't number it — an enormous number!

Asa's prayer when confronted with such an obstacle is one of the most beautiful in all of the Scriptures. He said, "LORD, there is no one like you to help the powerless against the mighty. Help us, O LORD our God, for we rely on you, and in your name we have come against this vast army. O LORD, you are our God; do not let man prevail against you" (14:11). Notice that Asa didn't beg. He didn't threat. He didn't say, "I," "me," or "my," like we so often hear in our prayers today. No! He simply placed his faith in the Lord. His heart was fully committed, and he knew that the Lord would come through. Notice also how much this sounds like David when he went up against Goliath. Both of these men realized that the battle was the Lord's, so their prayer reflected God's strength, rather than their circumstances. O, how much we can learn from people who have a heart for God.

You can pretty well predict the results of such faith. The Lord struck down the Cushites before Asa and Judah, so much so that the troops returned to Jerusalem with large amounts of plunder.

After this test the Lord sent the prophet Azariah to Asa. He reminded Asa that at one time Israel was in distress because they had no leader to show them God's ways, but now, with the people seeking Him, the Lord would be found by them. He also told Asa that his work would be rewarded.

REVIVAL COMES TO JUDAH

Asa was so encouraged that he decided to get even more serious about the spiritual needs of the people. He removed all the idols in the land, and repaired the altar in front of the Temple. Then he assembled all the people at Jerusalem for a great celebration. They sacrificed many animals, and rejoiced with shouting, trumpets, and horns. Then they made an oath to seek the Lord. Look at the devotion to God that came forth from all those present:

> They entered into a covenant to seek the LORD, the God of their fathers, with all their heart and soul. All who would not seek the LORD, the God of Israel, were to be put to death, whether small or great, man or woman. They took an oath to the LORD with loud acclamation, with shouting and with trumpets and horns. All Judah rejoiced about the oath because they had sworn it wholeheartedly. They sought God eagerly, and he was found by them (15:12-15).

Wow! This was serious business! If someone didn't go along with this covenant, they were to be put to death. Doesn't this seem a bit drastic? Well, it may seem drastic to us, but not to God, for back in Deuteronomy 17:2-7 He explained to all Israel that if someone violated their covenant with Him, they were to be taken out and stoned to death. He told them, "You must purge the evil from among you."

This seriousness did not slow down their excitement. They sought God, "*wholeheartedly*," and "*eagerly*."

In fact, Asa got so involved in this whole process that he had his grandmother, Maacah, deposed from her position as queen mother. Wow! Can you imagine going to your grandmother and telling her that because of her sin she would not be queen any longer. THIS MAN HAD A HEART FOR GOD!!! I suppose it could be argued that she should have been put to death for her rebellion towards God, but Asa stands out to me as one who would do whatever needed to be done for God's sake, regardless of what people might say. His "ONE AUDIENCE" was more important to him than all the others. Does this remind you of David?

Asa also, like David, brought into the Temple of God the silver and gold and the articles that he and his father had dedicated. His treasure was to bring glory and honor to his heavenly king.

TEST #2

Years after his first test, another one arose in Asa's life. Baasha, king of the northern country of Israel, built up the city of Ramah to shut off Judah. Ramah was on a main road in the center of the land between Israel and Judah. In effect, Judah was shut off from the north, with the desert to the south.

Asa came up with a great plan. He would take silver and gold from the treasuries of the Lord and his own treasuries and use these to make a treaty with Ben-Hadad, king of Aram (to the north). Ben-Hadad agreed, and sent his forces to attack Israel. The plan worked, for Baasha abandoned his work at Ramah. Asa and the men of Judah then took all of the building materials that had been left behind in Ramah and used it to build up their own cities.

What a plan! What success! Any entrepreneur today would be proud to put together a deal that worked out so favorably. But something was wrong! Remember what Asa did when he faced his first test? That's right, he prayed to God for victory. This time, in effect, he prayed to Ben-Hadad for victory. And where did all this money come from that he sent north to Ben-Hadad? Well, sure, some of it came from his own treasuries, but the rest of it came from God's treasuries. Asa's focus had changed since the covenant-making celebration of years past.

Isn't it interesting that the victories that we have in this life don't necessarily mean that we did things God's way. Yes, under our own power we can pull out some victories, but it doesn't mean that God is pleased with our methodology.

The Lord sent a prophet to Asa. He said, "Because you relied on the king of Aram and not on the LORD your God, the army of the king of Aram has escaped from your hand" (16:7). Yes, Asa was victorious over Israel, but with God's help, he would have conquered Aram also. O, how sad! We actually think that our victories amount to something, but when compared to the victories that we can have by placing our total dependence on God, they truly are meager. The prophet also told Asa that he had done a foolish thing, and that as a result, he would always be at war.

Here's where Asa fell apart. David would have accepted his discipline and known that it was best for him. But Asa's pride was too strong, for he threw the prophet in prison for what he had said. Then he brutally oppressed some of his own people. Asa eventually was afflicted with a disease in his feet. Two years later he died.

IN CONCLUSION

We can learn so much from the life of king Asa. We could look at the end of his life and learn more about the reap/sow principle. But, I think we should look at the positives in his life. We can see negative examples all around us. What we need is more positive examples of people who truly have a heart for God.

What did Asa do that made him truly a success? First, his heart was fully committed to the Lord. This has got to be the first step. To do any steps of obedience without a committed heart is like getting the cart before the horse. Our heart leads us to do those things that we know God wants us to do; things that will bring Him joy, and honor.

Then, Asa CLEANED UP THE SIN IN THE NATION. What sin do you need to clean up in your own life? Do you have a problem with anger, bitterness, greed, or sexual sin? How are your relationships with family, friends, and work associates? And what about your priorities? Do you have money, family, work, and God all in their proper place? Ask Him, "God, what would You have me clean up in my life?" You know what? He'll give you a clear answer.

Then, as Asa, SEEK AFTER GOD. Make your relationship with Him the most important part of your life. And finally, OBEY GOD'S LAWS AND COMMANDS. If you are willing to do these things, you'll see the great strength of God Himself leading you into victory in the battles of this life.

LESSON TWENTY-SIX

LESSONS LEARNED FROM STUDYING THE LIFE OF DAVID

David! The mere mention of that name brings many pictures to our minds. We see David as a boy tending his sheep. We see him under a tree playing his harp. We see him mightily slaying the giant, Goliath. We see him hiding in the cave from Saul. We see him on the throne, king over all Israel. We see him as a great warrior, leading his troops victoriously in battle. We see his sin with Bathsheba. We see him mourn the death of his son, Absalom. We see his evil census. And we see him pass on the torch to his son. But most of all, we see "*a man after God's own heart*."

David was not perfect. In fact, he was far from it. He was a rather normal, impetuous, strong-willed individual who made some terrible mistakes and dreadful choices in his life. But think about it for a moment. Isn't that the way we want the Scriptures to portray our Bible heroes? You see, if Abraham, Moses, or David, were represented as spiritually perfect, you and I could not relate to them at all. Their stories would not be relevant to us, because they were something special. Knowing that David struggled also, helps us to know that studying his life is very relevant for us, for we know how much we struggle with life. David had weaknesses! David faced temptation on a daily basis! He felt the inner war between good and evil! He knew real life — in all its positive and negative aspects alike. Yes, David was just like us. We can, and have, learned great lessons from studying his life.

In all his imperfection, however, David was used by God throughout the Bible as a sort of standard — a measuring stick for others in their "walk" with God. David's son, Solomon, was told that if he lived like David, he would be a success. And the following kings either "walked as their father David had done," signifying a righteous lifestyle, or they "did not walk like their father David had done," signifying their evil lifestyle. So, God took this man of many weaknesses and made him an example for us to follow today. Why? We've seen it clearly. Whenever David was confronted with his sin, he would repent. He wanted desperately to be close with his God, to be His companion. No matter what, his heart always brought him back to His God. David had a passion for his God. He was, after all, "a man after God's own heart."

LESSONS LEARNED

We've tried to define what it means to be a person "after God's own heart," yet a precise definition still eludes us. By reviewing some of the basic lessons that we have learned by studying David's life, perhaps it will more clearly define these words for us.

1) Our spiritual growth is a process, not a one time event (p. 9).

2) Our heart is our spiritual "epicenter." We should guard it very carefully (p. 13).

3) To obey is better than sacrifice (p. 16).

4) What is God looking for in our world today? Exactly what He was looking for in Saul's day — men and women after His own heart! This is not necessarily a perfect heart, but it is an honest, genuine, repentant heart! What about you? Where does your heart take you? What about your desires, your thoughts, your ambitions — the "real you"? Have you discovered some form of "heart disease" in your own life? Let the Lord have it! Spend quality time with Him so that He can create a new heart within you (pp. 16,17).

5) God does not see as man sees. He does not measure character by human charisma. He does not defer to human values. God's chief criterion for selecting special servants for mighty purposes is: "Are you willing to do My will?" This is the acid test (p. 19).

6) The practice of the spiritual disciplines will aid us greatly as we develop our "hearts for God" (p. 20).

7) It is important to realize that when a decision is made to truly give God our lives, the hassles and battles of life intensify. The Lord doesn't take us out of the battle, He simply gives us added strength (Himself) to stand strong under the barrage of life (p. 21).

8) Again and again, those who will dare to face the foe, to do battle with the forces of evil, find themselves harassed by their own family or friends (p. 22).

9) It doesn't matter what people think and say, if it opposes what God wants for our lives, because, it's really only ONE AUDIENCE that we live to please anyway (p. 23).

10) When up against a battle with giant proportions, keep your eyes on your covenant-keeping God and not your circumstances (p. 24).

11) Life throws things at us that we just don't understand. Things that we're not even sure that we can handle. Tough times! And yet Scripture is very clear that the purpose of these hard times is to help us to grow to be more like Christ, who "learned obedience from what he suffered" (Heb. 5:8, p. 28).

12) Be encouraged by the fact that David did not always have his eyes on God. This makes him just like us, not some perfect Bible hero that never was tempted. If he can become a "person after God's own heart," then so can we (p. 31).

13) We all need good Christian friends in our lives. Pray for one, and be one in turn. Make your relationship with God the basis of your relationship with others (p. 32).

14) When we set out to develop a heart for God, to serve Christ and His Church no matter what, it is not unusual to find a whole new set of problems — problems that were never expected. We may not understand. In fact, we may cry out to God for answers, as did David. But God is still on the throne, and He is allowing our trials to make sure that we still mean business, and to prepare us for future ministry opportunities (p. 33).

15) When facing trials, the decision is ours to make; am I going to be "bitter" or "better" as a result? (p. 36).

16) We cannot continue on in life with the philosophy which believes in "My Rights," or "Justified Retaliation." It's just not right! Pondering what it cost God to forgive us makes it much easier to consider forgiving someone who has wronged us (pp. 39,40).

17) Being a "man after God's own heart" doesn't mean we're perfect. No! It simply means that when we're confronted with our sin, we're willing to see it as God does and do what God would want us to do to take care of it (p. 41).

18) We cannot depend on past successes to get us through our current difficulties. We still have, and always will have, a sin nature which can raise its powerful head at any moment in our lives. We must always be alert! (p. 43).

19) Wait on the Lord, for He rewards every man for his righteousness and faithfulness (p. 46).

20) When feeling forgotten by God, share your thoughts and frustrations with Him so that He can help cure your broken heart (p. 49).

21) When we have peace in our lives, it doesn't necessarily mean that we've been obedient to God. Sin has its rewards, or else it would not be tempting. The question still remains — are we obedient, not just at peace? (p. 49).

22) When you hit "rock bottom," the only thing to do is to find strength in the Lord your God (p. 51).

23) Good intentions do not always lead to good results. We must be sure that we are living life God's way by inquiring of Him continually (p. 63).

24) God's "no" is not a rejection, but a redirection. The results depend on whether you "sulk" or "seek" (p. 66).

25) David and Mephibosheth showed us how to humbly deal with those who have been given authority over us (pp. 69,70).

26) Watch out for idle time. It can lead to great sins (p. 72).

27) Feeling rebellious? First, ask yourself what the Lord has done for you. Second, ask yourself if you despise God's Word, and God Himself. And, third, ask yourself how you feel when someone takes the Lord's name in vain (pp. 73-76).

28) When praying a prayer of confession: Pray for mercy, accept the responsibility for your sin, address your "One Audience," acknowledge that only God can cleanse you, and understand your responsibility to others (p. 77).

29) We must understand that our prayers of confession do not necessarily change the course of events that our choices set in motion (p. 78).

30) Parents, we must discipline our children with a balance of love and strictness (p. 80).

31) No matter how tough life becomes we can be confident that God has all things in control. Perhaps we are being disciplined, or perhaps we're being tested. But, through it all we can say with David, "It is good for me to be afflicted so that I might learn your decrees" (Psalm 119:71, p. 82).

32) The integrity of our leaders is of utmost importance in the Church today (p. 91).

33) We should not retire from the Lord's service in our older years, but continue with the passion of bringing Him glory and honor (p. 97).

34) David longed to leave behind him — in tangible form of stone, wood, gold, silver, and precious stones — a fitting sanctuary for the Most High. What do you plan to leave behind you when you leave this life? (p. 98).

35) David's final charge to Solomon showed his deep desire for the worship of God to continue in the life of his son. How do you "pass the torch" on to your children? (p. 99).

36) Live your life with passion! (p. 100).

37) God's incredible strength is always there, waiting for our hearts to be fully submitted and committed to His will. But, we must remember that it is a "cause-effect" relationship. When we are fully committed, it frees God to do mighty acts through us (p. 101).

38) A fully committed heart cleans up the sin, leads others in seeking the Lord, and commands others to obey God's Laws (p. 101).

39) David and Asa: both men realized that the battle was the Lord's, so their prayers reflected God's strength, rather than their circumstances (p. 102).

40) Isn't it interesting that the successes that we experience don't mean that we did things God's way. Yes, under our own power we can succeed, but it doesn't mean that God is pleased with our methodology (p. 103).

ONE FINAL CONCLUSION

God found David "a man after His own heart." What about you, and what about me? Could God say that of us? You know, it's our decision. We have all of the resources that David had. All we need to do is to "go for it!" Please join me, and countless other Christians around us who honestly strive to have God greet us one day with the words, "Well done, good and faithful servant, you are truly a person after My own heart!" God bless you in your passionate striving to please our only true "ONE AUDIENCE!"

REFERENCES

Allen, Ronald Barclay. *Praise! A Matter of Life and Breath.* Nashville: Thomas Nelson, 1980.

Bridges, Jerry. *The Pursuit of Holiness.* Colorado Springs: Navpress, 1978.

Briscoe, Stuart. *David —A Heart for God.* Wheaton: Victor Books, 1984.

Foster, Richard J. *Celebration of Discipline — The Path to Spiritual Growth.* San Francisco: Harper & Row, 1978.

Keller, W. Phillip. *David* (vol. 1) — *The Time of Saul's Tyranny.* Waco: Word, 1985.

_______. *David* (vol. 2) — *The Shepherd King.* Waco: Word, 1986.

Olsby, Gary. *Bible History Overview —Old Testament.* Joplin: College Press, 1990.

Pfeiffer, Charles F. *Old Testament History.* Grand Rapids: Baker Book House, 1973.

Redpath, Alan. *The Making of a Man of God.* Old Tappan: Fleming H. Revell, 1962.

Richards, Lawrence O. *The Teacher's Commentary.* Wheaton: Victor Books, 1987.

Schaap, Mary Nelle. *David's Lord.* Grand Rapids: Baker Book House, 1989.

Smalley, Gary, and John Trent. *The Language of Love.* Pomona: Focus on the Family, 1988.

_______. *The Two Sides of Love.* Pomona: Focus on the Family, 1990.

Swindoll, Charles R. *David —A Man After God's Own Heart.* Fullerton: Insight for Living, 1988.

Wilkinson, Bruce H, and Larry Libby. *Talk Thru Bible Personalities.* Atlanta: Walk Thru the Bible, 1983.